R. T. Kendall has a God-given talent for writing about the
right subject at the right time
fact that he writes profound,
and it is no wonder he is suc
book must be for everyone—
of their ministry, those who
leaders, and those who are trying to help fallen leaders.
This is a riveting read and will remain an important reference book for Christians from all backgrounds.

—**Lynn Green**
International Chairman
Youth With A Mission (YWAM)

Can God give second chances? Of course He can. RT
addresses the biblical blueprint for restoration in a very
thorough and thoughtful manner. It is not an automatic
process, however. It involves "godly sorrow" (2 Cor. 7:10)
and the grace of God that in turn produces a change of
mind and direction (true repentance).

There is a parallel, medically and physically speaking,
regarding the care of our bodies, God's sacred temple
(1 Cor. 3:17). Often a "physical fall" (stroke, heart attack,
heart failure, etc.) makes us finally change our minds
regarding long-standing unhealthy habits and addictions.
Admittedly, genetics can also play a big part.

I highly recommend this book for those who have fallen,
and hopefully, the principles herein will *prevent* falling as
well (Jude 24).

—**G. David Onstad, MD, FCCP**
Diplomate Internal Medicine
Pulmonary Disease, Critical Care, Geriatrics
Fort Lauderdale, Florida

As I read this manuscript, I was amazed how similar the
unfolding was to "Grand Rounds" during medical training
that preceded through history, examination, diagnosis,
treatment, recovery, and future prevention. I recommend

this work to physicians and other professionals in all fields of work because of the inherent traps related to sex, money, and power—epidemic in all elements and levels of society.

With bare knuckles, R. T. Kendall attacks the three most common causes of men and women falling from their spheres of influence, their fields of purpose, whether they be ministers, doctors, lawyers, teachers, public officials, or other workers of all sorts. The unholy etiological trio all produce warning symptoms of a coming fall. Dr. Kendall deftly pictures not only the progressive fall but also warning signals, measures of prevention, and means of recovery. Every stage is exampled in biblical heroes who have fallen and how they were restored.

This book's uncompromising encouragement for any who have fallen or are in the throes of such a downhill journey will be well worth reading and heeding.

I commend it to you without reservation, hesitation, or limitation.

—**Ira H. Slade, MD**
Internal Medicine
Griffin, Georgia

Dr. Kendall's book *God Gives Second Chances* is a foundational book for those of us who at one time or another had the feeling that we had built with wood, hay, or stubble. It brings scriptures together in an understandable way to promise us spiritual restoration.

As a layman somewhat limited in theological studies, I have had to trust in faith alone for my education. Being saved without a lot of knowledge has at times caused me a certain amount of confusion.

This book puts all the answers of restoration together in a concise manner with scriptures that reveal a loving Father, anxious to forgive and restore.

This book is an evangelistic book applicable to guilt-ridden church members who are desperately seeking a more meaningful ministry and a closer walk with Jesus. It reminds us that we have a loving Father who is not willing that any should perish in the future nor doubt in the present.

—**PETE CANTRELL**
PRESIDENT, AMERICAN ENERGY INC.
ADA, OKLAHOMA

At a time when there seems to be an epidemic of Christian leaders falling into sexual sin, R. T. Kendall's *God Gives Second Chances* speaks a powerful and timely word of healing, insight, and love. Although written primarily to give hope to the fallen, godly wisdom and counsel are dramatically presented to all who desire to finish well. This book is reminding us of "him that is able to keep you from falling, and to present you faultless before the presence of his glory with exceeding joy" (Jude 24). You would do well to read and digest it. I will be recommending *God Gives Second Chances* to all of us on our senior team, both as a resource as well as a life-giving warning.

—**JOHN ARNOTT**
FOUNDING PASTOR
TORONTO AIRPORT CHRISTIAN FELLOWSHIP

Dr. Kendall has again addressed one of the most important issues of our times with great power and clarity. This book is filled with profound and crucial insights about what is in fact a basic foundation of the faith but also one of the most neglected. This is a must-read for every Christian leader.

—**RICK JOYNER**
EXECUTIVE DIRECTOR
MORNINGSTAR CHURCHES AND MINISTRIES

GOD GIVES
SECOND
CHANCES

GOD GIVES SECOND CHANCES

R. T. KENDALL

Charisma
HOUSE
A STRANG COMPANY

Most Strang Communications/Charisma House/Siloam/
Excel Books/FrontLine/Realms products are available at
special quantity discounts for bulk purchase for sales promotions,
premiums, fund-raising, and educational needs. For details, write
Strang Communications/Charisma House/Siloam/Excel Books/
FrontLine/Realms, 600 Rinehart Road, Lake Mary, Florida 32746, or
telephone (407) 333-0600.

God Gives Second Chances by R. T. Kendall
Published by Charisma House
A Strang Company
600 Rinehart Road
Lake Mary, Florida 32746
www.charismahouse.com

Cover Designer: John Hamilton Design
                www.johnhamiltondesign.com
Executive Design Director: Bill Johnson

Library of Congress Cataloging-in-Publication Data:

Kendall, R. T.
  God gives second chances / R.T. Kendall.
     p. cm.
  Includes bibliographical references.
  ISBN 978-1-59979-253-8
  1. Repentance--Christianity. 2. Reconciliation--Religious aspects--Christianity. I. Title.

  BT800.K46 2008
  234'.5--dc22

                              2007032369

First Edition

08 09 10 11 12 — 987654321
Printed in the United States of America

What Others Are Saying About God Gives Second Chances

With his usual bare-knuckle candor and bottom-line clarity, R. T. Kendall has tackled a most delicate subject. All of us need to read it. You will find that the three groups he targets for readership will include us all: some who have fallen and have been found out; others who have fallen and are as yet not found out; and the rest who have sinned enough that their sins, if publicly known, would ruin their reputations.

Prepare to be shocked at how many have fallen.

Prepare to be confronted with the possibility that you may be the next one.

Prepare to be encouraged to know that it is impossible to be too careful with our emotional and spiritual lives.

Prepare to love those who have fallen, have been found out, and are struggling with a plethora of critical issues at this moment. While you are praying, pray for all of us. We all need it.

—Jack Taylor
President, Dimensions Ministries
Melbourne, Florida

Considered at any level, this is one of RT's greatest books. It might turn out to be the most important. For the backslider, it will bring great encouragement. For every Christian, it will inspire each of us to strive for high levels of love and purity. It gives much-needed help and advice concerning our sexuality, our handling money and power, and our need to stay confident and careful. I know of no book that is so deeply challenging in its call to the life of wholesomeness and holiness, yet it is without the "heaviness" and even oppressiveness that we associate with such themes.

In addition to its inspirational practicality, R. T. Kendall's work on the restoration of morally fallen Christians is an important work for other reasons, more so than one might perhaps think at first glance. The fourth century in the church was famous for establishing the deity of Christ; Athanasius was the great name. The early fifth century was notable for clarifying the grace of God. We think in this connection of Augustine of Hippo and his work. Anselm in the tenth century made some improvements in the doctrine of the Atonement. Luther brought to light justification by faith as never before. William Carey and Hudson Taylor were major thinkers behind the missionary movement. But the question we might want to ask is: when the history of the late twentieth and early twenty-first centuries are written (assuming the world survives long enough), what progress of doctrine will we associate with the period we are currently living in? Some of the answers to this question are already becoming clear. It has been a time when the *experiential* workings of the Spirit have been discussed more than ever. Calvin was clear and strong on the secret workings of the Spirit; the Pentecostal and Charismatic movements have driven us to consider the more *experiential* work of the Spirit, to which Calvin gave little thought. Massive church growth has taken place in areas of the church where evangelicals have accepted these doctrinal developments.

But there is another answer to our question. The period we are living in will surely become known as the time when the relationship and clear distinctiveness of justification over "inheritance" and "reward" is being clarified as never before. Suppose reward and justification are distinct, and suppose the great warnings of the Bible (notably the series in Hebrews 2:1–4; 3:7–4:13; 6:3–12; 10:26–39; 12:15–17, 25) are about reward and *not* about our unshakable "eternal redemption" mentioned in Hebrews 9:12 or our being "perfected for all time" as we see in Hebrews 10:14. Suppose Hebrews 10 refers to *reward* when it says, "If we go on sinning willfully after receiving the knowledge of the truth, there no longer remains a sacrifice for sins, but a terrifying expectation of judgment" (vv. 26–27). Suppose Hebrews 10:35 is simply continuing the theme when it says, "Do not cast away your confidence, which has great *reward*" (emphasis added). Then the way has been opened for a great and powerful doctrine of eternal security plus an immensely significant and forceful doctrine of loss and reward for the saved at the judgment seat of Christ.

This is the major forward step in theological thinking in the late twentieth century, done not so much by professors in universities or seminaries as by preachers leading churches who seek to motivate and inspire their people. There were many forerunners to this style of thinking, and a scholar studying at doctoral level a long time ago could insist that "Luther's unambiguous rejection of the doctrine of *merit* must not deceive us into thinking that the Reformer does not hold fast to the biblical sayings about reward." According to Luther, merit morality (*der schendliche Tück*) seeks its own honor, but the biblical reward teaching is different! It is full of grace. It allows for no pride. It makes us long to stretch forward to high levels of humble achievement in the kingdom of God. The modern forward step—increasingly being realized of distinguishing justification and inheritance—is only a small development of what has been Protestant teaching all along.

The next question to be considered is: how should this be preached? What is the practical outworking of this for the life of the churches? How should we *preach* reward and the fear (amidst exuberant assurance of salvation) of displeasing God? How can we *preach* Judgment Day *without* saying to our people, "You are maybe not *saved* after all"? It is at this point that RT's work is outstanding. There is a biblical doctrine of assurance. It is staggering in its power. It will lift us up to heaven. But there is also a fearful warning to any who wish to persist in extreme rebellion. It combines amazing encouragements for the scandalous backslider but fearful warnings of disgrace if rebellion continues. It is at this point we have RT's major contribution to the churches. Here we have a style of thinking and preaching that motivates us with ecstatic joy—and yet puts some sobriety in us at the same time. Here is "the fear of the Lord" without the endless doubts and trouble of conscience that beset any who go about to establish their own righteousness (Rom. 10:3). Here is theology on fire, theology at its best, theology that rescues the fallen. We might need it sooner than we think.

—**DR. MICHAEL EATON**
NAIROBI, KENYA

Does God give second chances? We know He does because the apostle Paul wrote, "Brothers, if someone is caught in a sin, you who are spiritual should restore him gently. But watch yourself, or you also may be tempted" (Gal. 6:1). This is good news because, as RT suggests, who among us hasn't fallen to one degree or another? Yet restoration seems to be one of the ministries that the church does not do very well. For example, people overtaken by an addiction—it may be a sexual addiction or a chemical addiction—usually end up going outside the church for help. There are, of course, Christian recovery groups within the church. But when they offer an annual conference, maybe two hundred people show up. When Alcoholics Anonymous hosts their annual conference, more than seventy thousand people show up. Who would have ever thought the church, with all its emphasis on the grace and power of God, would be so inept at leading alcoholics to restoration? Who would have ever thought that a group of recovering alcoholics referring to God as "your higher power" would do so much better at getting and keeping people sober?

After a member of my church attended her first AA meeting, she said to me, "I wish the church could be more like that."

"What do you mean?" I asked.

"Well, everyone was so real, and there was no judgment."

This is what every church member says after their first AA meeting. I've heard it many times now. And these words take us right back to Paul's words in Galatians 6:1. He said that the "spiritual" should do the restoring. But who are the spiritual? At a minimum, the spiritual ones are those who can restore the fallen *gently*. We can't restore the fallen gently if we are judging them at the same time. Jesus told us that would be like trying to take a speck out of someone's eye while we have a plank in our own eye (Matt. 7:1–5). To judge someone in this sense means that we feel superior to them. And when we feel superior to someone, we never fail to communicate that feeling. And who of us enjoys being around people who feel superior to us? Perhaps we have so little restoration in the church because we have so much judgment in the church.

"Everyone was so real," she said. I am haunted by those words these days. In the church the alternative to being real is being religious. Christ rescued me from an early and reckless death at age seventeen. My early Christian experience was real because my mentors were spiritual men. They were leaders in the youth parachurch movement called Young Life. I could talk to them about anything without fear of losing their respect or affection. I knew I would get the help I needed. And a young man being inundated with ever-increasing waves of testosterone needs a lot of help.

I finished college and got a new set of mentors, seminary professors. In my first few months at seminary, I had lunch with one of my professors. I was telling him about a sexual struggle I had had with my college girlfriend. I saw the pained look on his face as he changed the conversation to a benign subject. I thought, "Note to self, Jack: this is not an acceptable topic around here." So I started working on my image. One of the things I learned in seminary and my subsequent church experience was that I needed to appear better than I was. I wish someone would have told me that image management requires us to spend so much time both rehearsing and being on stage that there is very little time left over for real living. Religious people are actors and judges. They are not restorers.

People raised in a religious environment don't usually make very good candidates for restoration when they fall. They have been taught for so long to go underground with their sin that the light hurts their eyes too much. They don't realize how quickly the pain would pass if they would just walk out into the light all at once. But their devotion to the *image* of a holy person who has never existed holds them back. They have trusted that image to protect them rather than trusting the only true Protector. And they have seen what the judges did to others who fell.

What do you say to a person like this? How do you know if they have repented? How do you know if you have repented? What are some of the most common traps that cause people to fall? What is lost when we fall? R. T. Kendall addresses these questions and many more. He writes with the clarity and simplicity of one who understands both Scripture and history. This is the best book I've read on restoration. We need this book because we need to get better at restoration.

RT points out that even the righteous fall. Look at King David. But when the righteous fall, they rise again (Prov. 24:16). And the story of the prodigal son teaches us that our rising is more pleasing to our Father than our fall is displeasing. Perhaps if the church really believed this, we would see a lot less falling and a lot more restoring.

—JACK DEERE

To all those who need a second chance.

CONTENTS

Then the word of the LORD came to Jonah a second time.

—JONAH 3:1

Though you have made me see troubles, many and bitter, you will restore my life again.

—PSALM 71:20

A bruised reed he will not break, and a smoldering wick he will not snuff out.

—MATTHEW 12:20

But while he was still a long way off, his father saw him and was filled with compassion for him; he ran to his son, threw his arms around him and kissed him.

—LUKE 15:20

INTRODUCTION

WHEN OLIVER CROMWELL (1599–1658), KNOWN as the "Lord Protector" of England, viewed the portrait for which he had posed, he was offended. His face was seen with a perfect complexion, much like a modern photograph. "Where are the warts?" he asked. The reply was that the artist had removed them. Cromwell demanded that the portrait be repainted and presented to history "warts and all."

That is the way the Bible presents its heroes. The history of the Christian church is full of stories of people who have been truly converted but have grievously fallen. The same is true of the Old Testament. Unlike most modern biographies, the authors of Scripture present its heroes with "warts and all."

This book will have a good deal to say about the judgment seat of Christ. In a word, all *Christians* will face judgment—standing before the Lord Jesus Christ, "that each one may receive what is due him for the things done while in the body, whether good or bad" (2 Cor. 5:10). I will unpack this neglected teaching later on.

I remember having a long discussion with an old friend when I was the minister of Westminster Chapel. The issue: will *all* that is knowable about us be revealed to everybody at the judgment seat of Christ? My friend believes that *everything*—even our sins—will be revealed. When asked, "But what about the sins that have been washed away by the blood of Christ?" he replied that so were the sins of David and others who were clearly saved people described in the Bible. He then asked, "Why would everything David did be told and we get away with what we have done?" He reckoned that, as the Bible told the truth about Moses, Abraham, Jacob, David, Jonah, and others, hiding nothing, so too will all be revealed about us.

I believe he is wrong. I would not want you to find out all that is knowable about *me* at the judgment seat of Christ. Furthermore, I could easily make a good case against this unusual and sobering point of view. Total forgiveness, for example, means that *nothing* we have done that is wrong will be revealed to others at the judgment seat of Christ. But my friend believes that it will be the revelation of everything that all of us have done that will bring weeping at the judgment seat of Christ. "Why would there be tears at the Judgment if we are going to heaven?" I asked.

He answered, "God will say, 'This is what you did, but you are forgiven,' and this is when God will wipe away all our tears." (See Revelation 21:4.)

You may ask, if you don't believe such a point of view, why bring it into this book? I do it because his point of view made me think more soberly about this matter, and I think it was good for me that I do so. I think it will be good for you too, even if a shot across the bow that takes our breath away at the moment means we do not become overly familiar with holy things. As for me, it also makes me further appreciate, first, that all of us *will* stand before God at the judgment seat of Christ, and second, mercifully our sins will *not* be exposed, because they are washed away by the blood of Jesus.

Why is it that *some* Christians are exposed and judged in the here and now but others—who have done things that are equally scandalous and heinous in God's eyes—are not? Is the reason because those of us who have not been caught but who have made the angels blush are more godly, more worthy, more valuable, or more special than those who were found out? If

God judged the only person described in Scripture as the man after His own heart (1 Sam. 13:14; Acts 13:22), why do you think He would not judge you?

Tell me, have you not thought about this issue before?

When Paul said, "Knowing therefore the terror of the Lord, we persuade men" (KJV), it followed his statement, "For *we* must all appear before the judgment seat of Christ, that each one may receive what is due him for the things done while in the body, whether good or bad" (2 Cor. 5:10). This is clearly a reference to Christians. It is enough to scare us to death.

Martin Luther (1483–1546) said he expected three surprises when he got to heaven:

1. There will be those there he did not think would be there.
2. There will be those missing he was sure would be there.
3. That he will be there himself!

If I could borrow from Luther's observation, I too expect three surprises at the judgment seat of Christ:

1. There will be those who receive a *reward* that I did not think would get one.
2. There will be those who are *passed over* for a reward that I thought surely would receive one.
3. That I myself would receive a reward.

I have already written a book called *The Judgment Seat of Christ*[1] (originally published as *When God Says "Well Done"*), so I will not repeat all that is found there. But this book will nonetheless focus on certain principles in the New Testament about *preparation* for the final Judgment, especially looking at Paul's views in 1 Corinthians 3. Why should I bring in the judgment seat of Christ? It is because the lack of appropriate preparation for the final Judgment can result in God stepping in *now*—and judging those who did not take this preparation seriously.

I hold that there are two phases of the judgment seat of Christ:

1. God will separate the saved from the lost—the saved will go to heaven and the lost will go to hell.

2. God will call every single Christian who ever lived to give an account of the things done in the body, whether "good or bad"—some receiving a reward, others being saved by "fire" with no reward, as we will see below.

In a word, God will judge *all* of us in the *final Day* at the Judgment; He, for some reason, chooses to judge only *some* of us on this present pilgrimage on our way to that day.

It is hard to imagine *anybody* who can anticipate the judgment seat of Christ with glee and excitement. It would be a thousand times worse than waiting for the outcome of a verdict or an examination here below.

But when John talked about having boldness or confidence on the Day of Judgment (1 John 4:17) and being "unashamed before him at his coming" (1 John 2:28), I now breathe a sigh of great relief. I infer from this possibility that since my sins have been purified by the blood of Christ, they are therefore *truly buried* in the depths of the sea (Mic. 7:19), *not remembered* (Heb. 8:12), and separated from us "as far as the east is from the west" (Ps. 103:12), and you will not find out then all that could be known of me.

And yet this matter of standing before God Almighty at the judgment seat to give an account of the things done in the body—"whether good or bad"—is enough to send shivers down the spine of every soul. I simply do not want *you* to know what I know about me. I am counting on the blood of Jesus shielding you from the knowledge of what my sins were—not to mention God screening my family, my friends, and those to whom I have ministered over the last fifty years from knowing the total truth of all that God has graciously forgiven me of.

As to why some are judged in the here and now and others are not, I conclude two things:

1. The answer resides partly in these words: "I will have mercy on whom I will have mercy" (Exod. 33:19). It therefore lies in the mystery of God's inscrutable sovereignty. You and I should never forget this. Don't fancy yourself as being clever— or very important to God—if you don't get caught. That is foolish thinking.

2. But know also that nothing happens for no reason. God has a purpose in everything He does, doesn't do, or permits. If God rolls up His sleeves and openly judges one of His children in the present era, there is a good reason for it. After all, to those who love God, being called according to His purpose, there is a wonderful, wonderful promise: all things work together for good (Rom. 8:28).

There are probably no fewer than four categories of people reading this book:

1. You have never grievously fallen but fully realize your capabilities and know God to be merciful to you by dealing with you secretly by the internal chastening of the Holy Spirit and therefore have not (so far) given in to temptation.

2. You have indeed, sadly, succumbed to temptation—whether it be in reference to the sin of bitterness, self-vindication, damaging another's reputation, worldly things, money, sex, or power—but you have *not* been openly exposed (up to now).

3. You gave into one or more of these temptations but also *got caught*—and have been openly judged by the Lord so that your reputation has been hurt and your ministry or career has been, at least for a while, put in abeyance.

4. You have been shaken, perhaps disillusioned, by those you looked up to and who have fallen; it has made you wonder if you should give up ministry or going to church altogether.

It is impossible to say who among the four aforementioned categories needs this book more, so I hope to address all of these—whether ministers or laymen, high profile or low profile, even if those higher-profile Christians who have been publicly exposed seem to get more attention.

If *you*, then, have been exposed and have lost your ministry, job, and reputation, how do you feel? Are you bitter that you got caught? Do you feel it was unfair that someone *blew the whistle* on you? Do you feel that God has been unfair? Do you feel that the people who accused you also have skeletons in *their* closet—that it is grossly unfair that *they* be the ones who have pointed the finger? Or are you angry that there are others who have done the same thing—or worse things—and have continued on in business, practice, or ministry without any fear? So I would lovingly ask you, how do you feel that you have been openly judged?

I am reminded of a story my friend Rob Parsons shared with me. In one of the darkest hours of his life one Sunday morning, the well-known British preacher David Pawson unexpectedly knocked at his door. David began speaking to Rob about how painful it was for David to hear rumors going around about himself. But God spoke to David and said, "I know the *whole* truth, and the truth is worse than what they know; and I still love you." Then David Pawson gave Rob these words: "This too will pass, and the truth is worse than what they know." The comforting thought that *this too will pass* means that the immediate crisis will not last forever; God knows how much we can bear, and He has a way of enabling us to move on and then watch *Him* cause everything to work together for good (Rom. 8:28).

I say to every reader, whoever you are, in whatever category you may be in: The present situation will pass. And the truth is worse than what they know.

That things are not worse than they are is owing to the sheer grace and mercy of God.

I do know that when one church leader was exposed, he said that he was glad and that he thanked God for it. The exposure led to his repentance. You could therefore argue that it is God showing sovereign mercy in exposing us, however painful that must be. Indeed, I could make a very good case that times of special exposure are times of special mercy.

However, this book is not merely for ministers. Not at all. If you are what would sometimes be called a *layperson*—you are in business, in a profession, have a job, work outside the church and in a worldly environment—this book is for you. The truth is, a layman getting exposed and judged (unless he or she happens to have a very high profile in his church or community) gets less attention than that of a minister. But if you feel I have described *you* in any way here—and you know it—I plead with you to walk with me through this book. I say this because you too have to stand before God at the judgment seat of Christ to receive a reward for things done in the body, whether "good or bad."

And if you have been deeply hurt by watching your hero fall— or have been disillusioned by those you looked up to so highly— I pray that this book will come to you in the nick of time and that you will come through with a greater faith than ever.

We have all sinned to some degree—say, on a scale from one (minor—as in thoughts or words) to ten (major—as in thoughts, words, and scandalous deeds). Some argue that *sin is sin* and in the sight of God it doesn't matter how grievously one sins. Wrong. Some sins *are* worse than others. This is revealed by the various punishment for sin as meted out by the Mosaic Law (see especially Leviticus and Deuteronomy), not to mention that Jesus Himself talked about the "greater sin" (John 19:11) and stated that the punishment for some will be severer than for others (Luke 12:47–48). Some sins therefore bring greater dishonor to the name of our Most Holy God and are judged accordingly.

My first published book was on Jonah. I chose the Book of Jonah for my first series of sermons at Westminster Chapel in 1977. People asked why. I had one answer: "I am Jonah. I know what it is to be found out." It was why I felt I could preach from that book.

Have you ever been found out?

I have had the privilege of knowing a good number of great and famous men and women—church leaders and heads of state—and a few of them I got to know rather well. I learned a number of things, but one was (without exception) those people I began to admire a little bit too much sooner or later disappointed me. The more I had admired them, the greater the devastation when they let me down. A book I will never write could be titled *Great Men Who Disappointed Me and Why*. I pray nobody will write such a book about me. There are those out there who could do this! If people have let me down, I know that I have let others down.

My point is this. I do not write this book sitting on a high pedestal looking down at you. I will come clean with you; I write this book with fear and trembling.

The purpose of this book is partly to caution you if you have *not* fallen—lest you become self-righteous and think it can't happen to you.

I write also, as lovingly as I know how, to warn you if you have fallen but have not yet been judged for it—to urge you as earnestly as I know how to come to an unfeigned repentance.

I write to you if you are among that vast number of people who could not believe their ears when they heard of this or that person who had a moral failure of some sort. I hope you will not abandon the faith but will emerge as a spiritual giant and this growth might come partly from reading this book.

But I write mainly to encourage you if you have fallen—publicly or privately—especially if you fear you cannot be fully restored or used by God again. There will be some hard issues and passages of Scripture to face, and we will call a spade a spade. But to those who can "hear his voice" (Heb. 3:7), I can give categorical assurance: you can be used again, *warts and all*—just as those described in the Bible have been used again.

You are God's field, God's building.

—1 CORINTHIANS 3:9

And we are his house, if we hold on to our courage and the hope of which we boast.

—HEBREWS 3:6

In a large house there are articles not only of gold and silver, but also of wood and clay; some are for noble purposes and some for ignoble. If a man cleanses himself from the latter, he will be an instrument for noble purposes, made holy, useful to the Master and prepared to do any good work.

—2 TIMOTHY 2:20–21

The price of greatness is responsibility.

—WINSTON CHURCHILL (1874–1965)

CHAPTER 1

GOD'S HOUSE

I DON'T USUALLY REMEMBER THE TIME OR PLACE WHEN bad news comes my way. But I remember exactly where I was at 11:45 a.m. on October 9, 2004—in the Dallas-Fort Worth airport on our way to El Dorado, Arkansas. It was then that my friend Jack Taylor soberly relayed the news to me that our highly esteemed friend—a well-known preacher famed for his prophetic gift—had just been found guilty of homosexual sin. I was stunned and in shock for weeks. Although I had assumed I was one of his closest friends, I never suspected or dreamed that he could be doing anything like that.

If *you* are one who has fallen, you no doubt dreaded for others to hear of what you did. You thought of those who have admired you. You perhaps thought of those who were your personal enemies—who, sadly, might rejoice at your downfall. You have thought also about how hurt and shocked those close to you would be. Part of the pain of getting caught is the fear that people who never suspected your weakness would be disillusioned—not only with you but also with the gospel you have upheld.

Do you know what it is like to have such high esteem for someone—and then they let you down?

Can you imagine how the angels in heaven feel when the name of God is brought into disrepute by scandal in the church?

"The price of greatness is responsibility," said Winston Churchill. This is doubly true when it comes to Christian leadership. Not only that; the higher one's profile in the church—whether clergy or layperson—the greater the responsibility one has to maintain a godly walk. "Not many of you should presume to be teachers, my brothers, because you know that we who teach will be judged more strictly" (James 3:1).

As I said earlier, whether you are a layman or in ministry, I envisage four types of people reading this book, but I will mainly keep you in mind if you have fallen and you fear you cannot be used again. I would understand if you jumped ahead and read chapters you think are more relevant to you. If you must, turn to chapter 9, "Repentance." However, I would urge you not to do that but to read line by line what I have to say. Here is why: Those who do not learn from their past mistakes are doomed to repeat them. It is essential that you learn not only *what* went wrong but also why it went wrong. All I am writing is designed not only to give you hope for a brilliant future but also to ensure you do not fall again.

The purpose of this book generally, and this chapter particularly, is to help ensure that if you have fallen you don't repeat it, even if you are at this moment in a continued state of godly obedience. There are Christian psychologists who have cautioned that although a person has fallen and repented and appeared to be doing brilliantly, all too often that person lapsed into the same old malady within three to five years. In other words, doing well for a few months or even a few years is not good enough! When a person has overcome a bad habit and does well for a good while, the tendency is to think he or she is *cured*. Wrong. The weakness may always be there, and this is why too many have fallen after doing so well.

The purpose of this chapter is partly to introduce an important teaching that emerges in 1 Corinthians 3, namely, that our reward at the judgment seat of Christ will be based upon our personal lives as Christians—not our gifts, success, profile, or ability. Whether or not we receive a reward will be based entirely on our *character*. The truth about our character will be openly unveiled at the judgment seat of Christ.

Our reward at the judgment seat of Christ has everything to do with building a solid superstructure on the right foundation, which is what the apostle largely talks about in 1 Corinthians 3.

The church of which I was a part as I grew up in Ashland, Kentucky, always had twelve-day revivals three times every year—during autumn, winter, and spring. I myself had to be in church every single night of every one of them. They shaped my life and ministry, and I now thank God for those days. The best evangelists and preachers of my old denomination (Church of the Nazarene) were brought in. I had them on a high pedestal in my mind, and most of them deserved that admiration.

But I will never forget how I heard that one of them—possibly my favorite evangelist as I grew up—had been living in sexual immorality for years, even at the same time he was ministering to our church. It was revealed that a woman followed him wherever he went and managed to stay in the same hotel in which he was booked. What is more, he preached with as much power as I had ever witnessed. The way he could move people was amazing. A sense of the fear of God fell on the crowds as he spoke. He had such descriptive powers with language that when he preached on the subject of everlasting hell, for example, you could almost smell the brimstone. Dozens came forward night after night to be saved. There is no doubt that God used that man with many people, including me.

At the age of nineteen I first became a pastor of a church in Palmer, Tennessee. The district superintendent who put me there was one of my heroes. One Sunday morning in the spring of 1956 he showed up unexpectedly at my church. I was thrilled and asked him to preach. During his sermon I had an open vision. There to my astonishment was the Lord Jesus looking directly at him with utter disapproval. I could not understand it. I could not deny the vision, but it did not tally with what I knew about him. I never told anybody about this. What is more, I had to wait a long time to understand it. Ten years later it was revealed that he had been involved in an affair with a woman in Chattanooga, Tennessee, and was forced to resign as district superintendent. That affair was apparently going on when he preached for me.

People ask, How can a person's gift flourish when they are living in sin? I can only answer with Romans 11:29: "For God's gifts and his call are irrevocable"; "God does not change his mind about whom he chooses and blesses" (GNB); "The gracious gifts of God and his calling are irrevocable" (NEB). The Greek actually uses *ametameleta*—literally, God's gifts and calling are "without repentance" (KJV). This verse refers principally to God's own decree that He will not change His mind, but Paul is also saying that whether or not a person has repented of their sins is *not a necessary condition* for receiving or maintaining a spiritual gift.

Spiritual or ministerial gifts are sovereignly bestowed on a person, not because of one's good works or sanctification. This explains how King Saul, whom God had chosen but later clearly rejected (1 Sam. 10:1; 16:1; 18:12), still prophesied. Saul had been a given a change of heart along with the gift of prophecy (1 Sam. 10:9–10). But later, strange as it may seem, *on his way to kill young David*, "the Spirit of God came even upon him" and the people were still saying, "Is Saul also among the prophets?" (1 Sam. 19:23–24; cf. 1 Sam. 10:11). God's approval had been withdrawn but not Saul's gift.

Saul's example also explains how the aforementioned evangelist I admired, as well as my old district superintendent, could preach with effectiveness and be such a hypocrite. This of course provides a theological rationale as to how the fallen TV evangelists in the 1980s could carry on in their private lives without pure hearts and yet mesmerize their followers—and even be used of God.

But having an irrevocable gift does not mean that one is exempt from God's severe displeasure and judgment. A gift from God is bestowed upon the assumption that one will not abuse such a privilege. One should be utterly grateful to God for his or her talent, anointing, natural ability, calling, and following. If they are not full of gratitude, which is demonstrated by words and deeds, those same people will sooner or later be found out and will also discover that the effectiveness of that gift diminishes.

As for King Saul, he eventually lost everything, including any connection with anything prophetic. "God has turned away from me. He no longer answers me, either by prophets or by dreams," lamented Saul near the end of his life (1 Sam. 28:15). I would suspect therefore that a person's gift can flourish for a while despite that person's conduct, but eventually that gift will begin to disappear if the person is not finally granted unfeigned repentance. Therefore, the irrevocability of one's gift should not be regarded as meaning that it will be *effective* forever.

As a matter of fact, when I reflected on the aforementioned fallen preacher with the unusual prophetic gift, I realized he had begun to prophesy with less and less accuracy, especially regarding future events. Whereas he was once known to have a very high degree of accuracy (John Wimber personally told me he never knew this man to get it wrong), that began to change at some point. He began to miss it a lot. For example, during one of my last visits with him he emphatically stated to me that George W. Bush would be a "one-term president"—but Bush was in fact reelected. That was a pretty big miss. I am therefore saying that a person's gift may flourish for a while when they are living in sin but not be effective forever.

JUDGMENT ON GOD'S HOUSE

Why does God step in and judge some but leave others to continue in their sin? It has mostly to do with God's sovereign and inscrutable purposes but also His infinite patience. And yet the answer may also have something to do with how angry He is, in which case He may prefer to wait and deal with some disobedient servants at the final Judgment. However, all sin will be judged sooner or later—whether in this life or at the judgment seat of Christ.

The apostle Peter stated that judgment "must begin at the house of God" (1 Pet. 4:17, KJV; "family," NIV). This is because God has chosen to delay judging the world generally until He has first called His own people particularly to give an account regarding their covenant responsibility. He therefore starts the process of judgment with His elect people first.

He often begins with those in leadership. Why? Because leaders are supposed to *lead*—not follow—both by a higher level of wisdom and also by example. They are not to be as it was once said, "Like people, like priests" (Hos. 4:9), that the priests mirrored the people's unjust wishes and ungodly example.

Leaders were to be different. *Like priest, like people,* assuming the priest is of impeccable integrity, character, and reputation, is the way it should be.

But when the leaders go wrong, the people go wrong. It filters from the top on down. When the leaders do not uphold God's standard, the people will not have a sense of direction. God judged Eli the high priest before He judged the people of Israel generally (1 Sam. 4). Moreover, as I stated, those who are teachers—or leaders—will be judged more strictly (James 3:1).

When Peter said that judgment must begin with the house, or family, of God, I don't think he was referring to an order of events at the final Judgment, although it could imply that. If so, it could therefore suggest that the *saved* will be dealt with before the lost are held accountable at the final Judgment. However, I think Peter's statement that judgment must begin with the family of God refers to the way God has chosen to deal with His own people in the *here and now*—in advance of the final Judgment.

We must never forget this incontrovertible fact: We are *all* going to face God's final Judgment. We should live our lives accordingly. That is one of the reasons that the Bible *tells* us there is a coming judgment—to change our lives *now* and so to prepare us for that frightening event.

But it is equally true that God can give us a *taste* of the final Judgment in advance of that day. As a matter of fact, good preaching on the subject of the final Judgment should do this. When the reality of eternity is brought home so that it invades the present, the people will sense the fear of God and even feel something of what it will be like on that day.

And yet a foretaste of the final Judgment is what is actually taking place when you read of certain people who have been *caught*—for it is what *God* did. People who are being exposed like this is no accident; it is what God does. It is judgment in advance of the Judgment. When Paul says that if we judge ourselves, we will not be judged (1 Cor. 11:31), referring to the Lord's Supper, he is telling us that you and I can be spared of this judgment below and the final Judgment if we deal with sin in the here and now. Dealing with our sin in the here and now means acknowledging it, not denying it, and repenting of it.

On the other hand, it could be more painful to be found out *then* at the judgment seat of Christ than to be exposed *now* in advance of the Judgment. There is an observable pattern in the history of God's dealings with His people: the angrier God is, the longer He sometimes waits before showing His ire. However painful it must be to be caught and judged here below, it will be worse then.

USES OF *HOUSE* IN SCRIPTURE

The Greek word *oikou*, "house" in 1 Peter 4:17, is translated "family" of God in the NIV. The word *house* is used in multitudinous ways in the Bible. For example, it may refer to a physical structure or superstructure above a foundation. It may refer to God's manifest presence. It may refer to people, among other uses. The first time the word *house* occurs in the Bible is when God said to Noah, "Come thou and all thy house into the ark" (Gen. 7:1, KJV), translated "family" in the NIV.

The first time the phrase "house of God" occurs in the Bible is when Jacob woke up after his dream of the angels and said, "Surely the LORD is in this place, and I was not aware of it.... How awesome is this place! This is none other than the house of God; this is the gate of heaven" (Gen. 28:16–17).

I have been amazed to see how vast the subject of *house* is in the Bible. The word *house* itself appears no fewer than two thousand times—but is used, as I said, in many different ways. House therefore can refer not only to people or a building, but also the temple: "My house will be called a house of prayer" (Matt. 21:13).

In 1 Corinthians 3, as we will see in some detail, Paul will talk about *you* and *me* being a *building*—what we today would call the superstructure over a foundation (v. 9). We, God's people, are His "building" and are thus temples of the Holy Spirit (1 Cor. 3:16).

And that is what Hebrews 3:6 means, quoted at the beginning of this chapter: "We are his house"—God's house, dwelling place, building, or superstructure.

It is a sobering but thrilling privilege to be called God's *house*. For that is what you and I are. God has put us on our honor to build that house, or superstructure, in accordance with our Architect's glorious blueprint. As the tabernacle in the wilderness was to be a copy of the real temple in heaven (Exod. 25:40), so are you and I intended to be God's house, as He has willed for us in heaven.

In 1 Corinthians 3 Paul tells us what the ingredients, or materials, of this house are to be made of. We are presented with two possibilities—two sets of materials (v. 12):

1. Gold, silver, precious stones
2. Wood, hay, straw

Paul states it in much the same way to Timothy: "In a large house there are articles not only of gold and silver, but also of wood and clay; some are for noble purposes and some for ignoble" (2 Tim. 2:20). This means that the same house can be a mixture of the good, the bad, and the ugly. Our mandate is to be cleansed from what is ignoble in order that we may be instruments for "noble purposes, made holy, useful to the Master and prepared to do any good work" (v. 21). When we have been cleansed in this manner, we will therefore build God's house wisely with the materials that bring Him honor and glory. But if we are not so cleansed, we will foolishly erect a superstructure of materials that will be burned up on the Day of Judgment. And, as I said, God may expose us in advance of that day.

WISDOM AND SEXUAL PURITY

When I said it is no "accident" that a person is found out, I need to make two observations:

1. In His own sovereign time and manner, God decides to roll up His sleeves and judge, as He did with King David (2 Sam. 12). God simply stepped in and did what He felt He had to do.

2. It is not an accident but predictable when a person falls grievously. It didn't just "happen," although it may appear that way. For a grievous fall is the consequence of a failure to prepare adequately for the test, to which I will return below.

Let me address you if you are one who has not only fallen but somehow got caught. I risk saying things that can make you feel guilty. It is the last thing I want to do, believe me. You already have enough guilt on your plate; I have no desire to add to that. The problem is, when I point out the ingredients that make for a superstructure with gold, silver, and gems, you may get the feeling that you are reading this "too late." So why should you read this?

I answer: Because there is hope. There is time. It is not too late. For any teachable person who has fallen, God would not put this book in your hands to condemn you or give you no hope. You can begin *now* to rebuild your superstructure. I will have a lot more to say on this when we take a look at the life of David below. In the meantime, if your attitude is one of wanting to get it right from this point, all I write, I can assure you, is aimed to help you, not make you feel "if only I had done that."

In other words, if you don't "dig in your heels" as some have done when they were exposed, God can use you again. My loving suggestion: welcome the disciplining of the Lord as you would an honored guest. If you do this, you will heal inwardly and outwardly, and God can make things happen for you and use you again. "Though you have made me see troubles, many and bitter, you will restore my life again; from the depths of the earth you will again bring me up. You will increase my honor and comfort me once again" (Ps. 71:20–21).

But if you resent the fact that you got caught, and point the finger at whoever *blew the whistle* on you, refusing to accept the counsel of those in authority over you, you will never, never, never come back.

When I think of certain leaders, some of them being my friends, who were exposed in recent years, and I observed their reaction (refusing to accept wise advice and loving discipline), my heart aches. I often think of those who could be back in the place of strategic ministry today but who will remain yesterday's men and yesterday's women. Why? Because they refused to accept the discipline that was required by those who were willing to help them. For some, then, I fear it is too late.

But not for you. That is why I write this book. So bear with me in what I say. Not a single word is designed to give you a heavy, guilty feeling but only a light sense of God's beckoning to put things right.

Our whole lives can be called *preparation for a test.* Like it or not, we are, day and night, always erecting a superstructure. That is why we are called "God's house." The important issue is our daily choice of materials for the house we are building. If, for example, you and I choose wood, hay, straw, or clay when building the superstructure, we are setting ourselves up for an inevitable crash; our fall is predictable. If on the other hand we choose to erect a superstructure with gold, silver, and gems, we will not likely fall here below, neither will we be ashamed at the judgment seat of Christ. I will explain later how these metaphors are to be applied.

It may surprise you to see how closely wisdom and understanding are connected to sexual purity. You see it again and again in the Book of Proverbs. Early on in this amazing book of Scripture we learn that "the fear of the LORD is the beginning of knowledge, but fools despise wisdom and discipline" (Prov. 1:7). Wisdom is what saves one "from the adulteress, from the wayward wife with her seductive words" (Prov. 2:16). (See also Proverbs 5:1–14, 20–23; 7:1–27.)

> How long will you simple ones love your simple ways? How long will mockers delight in mockery and fools hate knowledge? If you had responded to my rebuke, I would have poured out my heart to you and made my thoughts known to you. But since you rejected me when I called and no one gave heed when I stretched out my hand, since you ignored all my advice and would not accept my rebuke, I in turn will laugh at your disaster; I will mock when calamity overtakes you—when calamity overtakes you like a storm,

when disaster sweeps over you like a whirlwind, when
distress and trouble overwhelm you.

—PROVERBS 1:22–27

It can be summed up in this verse: "A man who commits
adultery lacks judgment; whoever does so destroys himself"
(Prov. 6:32). Consider how the proverbs repeat themselves:
"Say to wisdom, 'You are my sister,' and call understanding
your kinsman; they will keep you from the adulteress, from the
wayward wife with her seductive words" (Prov. 7:4–5).

What I have quoted in the previous paragraph can be summed
up: If one rejected the fear of the Lord, which is the beginning of wisdom and understanding, his or her fall as a result of
sexual temptation is not a case of *surprise, surprise*. It was only
a matter of time. Furthermore, falling into sexual sin is not only
foolish; it causes one to forfeit the promise of a greater understanding. Speaking personally, I *live* for understanding, wisdom,
and insight. One of my greatest fears is that I might accept or
pass on any doctrinal error. Falling into sexual sin removes my
hope that God will give me insight from His Word.

To put it another way, choosing the correct materials for
building God's house is a way of preventing sexual sin. Rejecting
the ingredients that erect a faulty superstructure (wood, clay,
hay, straw) is what Paul means by being *cleansed* from dishon-
orable motives so that we are instruments of "noble purposes,
made holy, useful to the Master and prepared to do any good
work" (2 Tim. 2:21).

However, building God's house with clay or straw does not
only refer to sexual matters; we will see that the superstructure
covers the whole of our lives—our bodies, souls, and spirits. But
because so much, sadly, that pertains to a grievous fall relates to
a moral failure, we must give due attention to this area.

We—you and I—are God's house. "Unless the LORD builds the house, its builders labor in vain" (Ps. 127:1). This amazing verse mainly refers to our embarking on a project that God is not *in*, in order to show the folly of trying to build what is not His idea. In a word, it won't work! But when it comes to our building the superstructure, you can be sure that God is behind our selection of the right materials. He does not want a superstructure that will not stand the test. So remember: in building God's house, this is something He is *in*, and you have Him behind you all the way.

Well done, good and faithful servant! You have been faithful with a few things; I will put you in charge of many things. Come and share your master's happiness.

—MATTHEW 25:23

Therefore, my brothers, be all the more eager to make your calling and election sure. For if you do these things, you will never fall, and you will receive a rich welcome into the eternal kingdom of our Lord and Savior Jesus Christ.

—2 PETER 1:10–11

For I am already being poured out like a drink offering, and the time has come for my departure. I have fought the good fight, I have finished the race, I have kept the faith. Now there is in store for me the crown of righteousness, which the Lord, the righteous Judge, will award to me on that day—and not only to me, but also to all who have longed for his appearing.

—2 TIMOTHY 4:6–8

Best of all, God is with us.
—THE LAST WORDS OF JOHN WESLEY (1703–1791)

CHAPTER 2

ENDING WELL

THE OLDER I GET, THE FASTER TIME FLIES; THE OLDER I get, the more I cry out to God, "Let me end well."

I have been amazed at the number of church leaders who did not end well either because of a moral failure or a spiritual deficiency. Sometimes a sad deathbed state comes from lack of assurance of salvation, as in the case of the great Puritan preacher William Perkins (1558–1602). Strange as it may seem and godly though he was, Perkins spent much of his preaching life stressing assurance of salvation, but he died without it himself. A large part of my Oxford thesis centered on Perkins's emphasis of 2 Peter 1:10, "Make your calling and election sure."

William Perkins taught that assurance of salvation was to be based on godly living, but he actually died not knowing for sure if he himself was truly saved. I would hate to die like that. It was not that he became less than godly in the end. No, it was because he was a victim of his own theology. He put the ground of assurance on such a high level that knowing you were saved was out of reach for most people. He insisted that assurance of salvation came through the maintenance of sanctification, or good works. Such sanctification was to be based upon carefully keeping the Ten Commandments and the Sermon on the Mount. This observance must be exhibited day and night in thought, word, and deed. The basis of assurance of salvation not only became beyond the grasp for so many of his followers but even for Perkins himself.

When I first came to Westminster Chapel I was continually surprised by the number of good people who would come into the vestry (pastor's study) after a sermon and say that my own preaching gave them hope that they were truly converted after all! "What?" I would say to them, "Here you are, a professing Christian for all these years, and you have not been sure that you will go to heaven when you die?" Sadly, that was too often the case. It was not a matter of moral scandal in their private lives but a theology that put assurance out of reach for conscientious people. Many of these people were avid readers of the Puritans' writings. Some of them were theologically acute but spiritually deprived.

But far worse would be coming to the end of one's life and being remembered almost entirely for a moral failure, a lack of integrity, or to have been involved in a financial scandal. It is like Watergate with Richard Nixon or the moral failure of Bill Clinton. People like this will not be largely remembered for good things they no doubt did when in the White House. In any case, so many brilliant lives in the secular world and in the church ended under a cloud. What is more, such people come from every conceivable theological and church background. I am talking about Evangelicals, Fundamentalists, Reformists, Baptists, Presbyterians, Nazarenes, Methodists, Episcopalians, Anglicans, Pentecostals, and Charismatics. There is *no* theology that can guarantee transparent character if the person does not want to honor God in his or her life day and night. It has happened to the best of men and women. It could happen to you and me.

As for you, it is not too late for you to end well.

In this book I will quote more than once the man I was named after, Dr. R. T. Williams. When ordaining people to the ministry, he would exhort: "Young men, beware of two things: money and women; because if your ministry is characterized by a scandal regarding either of these, God will forgive you but the people won't."

The apostle Paul ended well. He said so in what was almost certainly his last epistle when he wrote to Timothy: "I have fought the good fight, I have finished the race, I have kept the faith. Now there is in store for me the crown of righteousness, which the Lord, the righteous Judge, will award to me on that day" (2 Tim. 4:7–8). He did not have such confidence early on, for he said to the Corinthians, "I beat my body and make it my slave so that after I have preached to others, I myself will not be disqualified for the prize" (1 Cor. 9:27). This was written around A.D. 50. But some fifteen years later he could say to Timothy, just before he was beheaded in Rome, that he would receive the crown to which he aspired. He was not worried about whether he was saved when he wrote those words in 1 Corinthians 9:27; he was very concerned that he not be rejected for the prize—a reward that is offered in addition to salvation.

Rewards will be handed out at the judgment seat of Christ. I have heard people say, "I don't care about getting a reward after I die; I just want to make it to heaven." I don't mean to be unfair, but I have never thought a comment like this reflected a very deep spirituality. It sometimes even smacks of false modesty, as in the old song I heard as I grew up, "Lord, Build Me a Cabin in Glory"—as if one did not want a spectacular mansion, only a cabin! The truth is, although I don't know precisely what a reward in heaven entails (other than God saying, "Well done"),

I know it was of deep concern to Paul who wanted it almost more than anything, and who could say in the end that he *got it.*

This brings the importance of the judgment seat of Christ before us. It cannot be stated too firmly or too often that one of the main reasons we have this very teaching in the New Testament is not only to show that God will have the final word, but that, knowing we will stand before the Lord Jesus Christ on the last day, the anticipation of this event might *change our lives in the here and now.* That is why Paul added, "Knowing therefore the terror of the Lord, we persuade men" (2 Cor. 5:11, KJV). He included himself, as well as you and me, when he stated, "We must all appear before the judgment seat of Christ, that each one [of us] may receive what is due him for the things done while in the body, whether good or bad" (2 Cor. 5:10). This is not a reference to the judgment of the lost who go to hell but what happens to the saved.

In a word, saved people will have to give an account of the things done *while in the body.* The reward will therefore be based on how you lived on Earth.

I find it so interesting that the same apostle Paul who spent much of his life stressing justification by faith alone and salvation by sheer grace also had the most to say about a *reward* at the judgment seat of Christ! That is why Paul said, "I beat *my body* and make it my slave" (1 Cor. 9:27, emphasis added). Why? Not because he thought he had to do that to make it to heaven. After all, salvation is by grace apart from works (Eph. 2:8–9). Paul's fear, therefore, was not missing heaven but being rejected for the "prize." In other words, he was not talking about whether he may or may not get into heaven; he was talking about something *in addition* to going to heaven—or you could say *in advance* of getting to heaven—a reward at the judgment seat of Christ on the last day.

We should know therefore that Paul was not the slightest bit worried about being rejected for entrance into heaven. It was the *prize* he was worried about. The word *prize* (Greek *brabion*—used also in Philippians 3:14) is used interchangeably with *crown* (Greek *stephanos*—used eighteen times in the New Testament) and *reward* (Greek *misthos*—used twenty-nine times), and often with *inheritance* (Greek *kleronomia*—used at least seventeen times as meaning "reward," as in Colossians 3:24).

One of the clearest but most neglected teachings in the New Testament is the distinction between salvation and *reward*. All who rest on the foundation, namely, Jesus Christ (1 Cor. 3:11), will be saved. They are assured of heaven. That is *given* to us; it is a free gift (Rom. 6:23). But not all who are saved will receive a *reward* (1 Cor. 3:14–15), which we will see in more detail below.

It was the *reward*, then, that Paul was after. He could not bear the thought of seeing others get a reward, then he himself be rejected for this reward, crown, or prize. But he knew this was possible. He dreaded the shame of being openly rejected for this prize more than anything. That is why he kept his "body" under subjection (1 Cor. 9:27).

What the King James Version translates "castaway" in 1 Corinthians 9:27 and translated "disqualified for the prize" in the NIV comes from the Greek *adokimos*, which means "rejected." The fuller meaning of *adokimos* means "tested, but not approved." The Hebrew equivalent is used in Jeremiah 6:30: "They are called rejected silver, because the LORD has rejected them." All of us will be tested by fire on that day. But not all of the saved will be approved. This is because some saved people did not end well; their works will be burned up.

Paul knew this could happen to him. I know it can happen to me. Do you realize it can happen to you?

Speaking personally, I don't know of any doctrine in Scripture that has had greater impact on me than this. Frankly, I myself am not worried about being eternally lost; I *do* worry about being rejected for the "prize" at the judgment seat of Christ, the very thing Paul was concerned about. This motivates me to live a transparent, pure, and godly life more than I can possibly describe. It is before me all the time. It pulls me forward; it keeps me on my knees and mercifully has kept me from succumbing to temptation when I might have given in. What is more, like Paul, I know that my converts and those who have listened to me and read my books will *see for themselves* whether I am genuine or phony on that day.

SOME OF MY FEARS

Let me share some of my deep fears with you. I have them. I am talking about honest concerns that worry me when I think of ending well.

1. I fear that God would take His hand off me and leave me alone.

I am reminded of those ominous words, "Ephraim is joined to idols; leave him alone!" (Hos. 4:17). I cannot think of anything worse than for God to leave me alone. It is said of those who rejected the knowledge of creation clearly revealed to the conscience, that God merely "gave them over" (Rom. 1:24, 26). As my old friend Rolfe Barnard used to say, "Paul didn't say that God *clubbed* them or *pushed* them; He just *gave them up*."

The psalmist dreaded God's "hot displeasure" (Ps. 38:1, KJV), but C. H. Spurgeon implied that there was something worse than that—God's cold shoulder: "Who can stand before his cold?" (Ps. 147:17, KJV). That is when God *ceases to deal with a person.* It is precisely what Hebrews 6:4–6 means by a person who cannot be renewed again to repentance.

Some time ago, Billy Graham said that his worst fear was that God would take His hand off him. It is my fear too. It can't get worse than that. But it is exactly what happened to King Saul, as I said earlier. Let me remind you: Here was a man who was chosen of God (1 Sam. 9:15–16), who had a brilliant beginning (1 Sam. 10:9–10), who lost the anointing of God's approval (1 Sam. 16:1; 18:12), and yet whose prophetic gift flourished simultaneously with his shameful behavior (1 Sam. 19:18–24). This was Saul on his way to kill young David because David was such a threat, and yet Saul prophesied as if he still had God's total favor.

In other words, King Saul's gift flourished as if all was well and as though his relationship with God was as it once had been, as if nothing bad had happened in the meantime.

It reminds me of that terrifying statement by the Episcopal rector some years ago who said that if the Holy Spirit were taken completely from the church today, 90 percent of the work of the church would carry on *as if nothing had happened.* That can happen to a church; it can happen to an individual. It is what happened to Saul and what could happen to you and me. This is the kind of theology the apostle Paul was immersed in. It explains his fear of being "disqualified for the prize" in 1 Corinthians 9:27. The Hebrew equivalent of the Greek word we looked at above—*adokimos*—is used of King Saul: "I have rejected him as king" (1 Sam. 16:1). But Saul continued on as if nothing had happened.

It is so easy for either a God-given, natural ability or a gift of the Holy Spirit, as in 1 Corinthians 12:7–11, to camouflage our true, secret relationship with God.

2. I fear that I might teach what is not exactly true.

I cannot bear the thought that I would pass on any measure of theological error. I suppose some people do not worry too much about whether they hold to sound theology. But I do. It is my life. I want to get it right in my thinking before I stand in a pulpit or take pen in hand. I will have to give an account of every sentence I have written, every word I have uttered (in and out of the pulpit), including every "careless" word (Matt. 12:36).

What is my assurance that I will not accept or teach heresy? One thing—my obedience to the Holy Spirit. My guarantee of sound theology does not come from my training, my mentors, my reading, or my level of intelligence; it is the result of my unconditional obedience to the will of God. I put all my eggs into this basket—Jesus's words: "If any man will do his will, he shall know of the doctrine, whether it be of God, or whether I speak of myself" (John 7:17, KJV). I do not say that this verse promises to deliver a perfect theology to all who aspire to do God's will, whether or not they are trained or well read. But I do think it promises to keep us from any *serious* theological error—certainly when it comes to Christology—when our relationship with God is right.

Here is why. If I have not grieved the Holy Spirit through bitterness (or whatever else grieves Him—see Ephesians 4:30–5:7), I can expect to have full benefit of the promise from Jesus that the Holy Spirit will guide me into "all truth" (John 16:13). When I grieve the Spirit, the anointing temporarily lifts, and I cannot think so clearly during this time or enjoy all the benefit of the promises that pertain to the Holy Spirit, as in John 14–16.

But when I am granted repentance and am changed from glory to glory (2 Cor. 3:18), I am given insights that are good, solid, and true. To be honest, it is what I live for. Nothing—absolutely nothing—thrills me more than a fresh insight that comes from the immediate and direct work of the Holy Spirit. I therefore fear that I might somehow imagine I have an insight from Him, when it is actually of the flesh. No theologian, however godly, learned, or honest, is infallible.

I hang fast, however, on doing the will of God by not grieving the Holy Spirit.

3. I fear that I could be out of the will of God and not know it.

If this could happen to Joseph and Mary, it could happen to you or me. They went an entire day without Jesus but assumed the whole time "he was in their company" (Luke 2:44). I based my book *The Sensitivity of the Spirit* largely on this account.[1] It is so easy to take the will and presence of God for granted.

I am sobered when I recall that God is no respecter of persons, that He will not bend the rules for any of us. If Joseph and Mary, Jesus's own parents, could run ahead of Jesus, proceeding without Him when they sincerely thought He was with them, then you and I could do this. But if we do it, we too will have to go to the same lengths to find Jesus as they did (Luke 2:45–50). If we proceed without Him, then we too are *on our own.*

The only prevention I know of is to develop an intimate knowledge of the *ways* of the Holy Spirit. The more familiar I am with His presence and His ways, the more likely I will *instantly sense His absence* when I move ahead without Him.

To be fair, I don't think anyone whose heart longs for His presence can get *seriously* out of God's will for very long. But I do not want to go a day, not even an hour, knowingly, without His conscious presence.

4. I fear that I might discover that I could have had much more of God and be used in a greater manner but for my stubbornness to recognize His warnings.

I have made so many mistakes over the past fifty years. I would give anything to have a second chance in certain areas (especially with my family). I know I am a forgiven man. I have forgiven myself—totally, as I say in *How to Forgive Ourselves—Totally*.[2] Furthermore, I hang on to Romans 8:28 (KJV): "And we know that all things work together for good to them that love God, to them who are the called according to his purpose." I believe in that promise with all my heart.

But I admit at the same time that I sometimes wonder how much better it might have been had I listened to clear cautions from the Lord over the years. This is why I am so keen not to brush aside any loving word from a friend or stranger—lest I miss all that God would do with me. The older you get, the more you want to avoid any past mistakes.

5. I fear that I might not hear God say to me, "Well done."

You may say that all Christians get that very same commendation when they get to heaven. But I don't agree. A "rich welcome" is promised on certain conditions (2 Pet. 1:11, ASV). This is one of several reasons I hold that not all who go to heaven get the same reward or that all will even get at least *some* reward. As we will see further below, only those who built a superstructure made of gold, silver, and costly stones will receive a reward. Those who built a house made of wood, hay, or straw will have their whole superstructure "burned up"; they will "suffer loss" (of reward), but nonetheless "will be saved, but only as one escaping through the flames" (1 Cor. 3:14–15).

As for those people who say, "I don't care about a reward, I just want to make it to heaven," I know what they mean by that. After all, the difference between heaven and hell is infinite and incalculable. Those who are spared eternal punishment and make it to heaven have a debt to God that can never be paid. It was paid by the blood of Jesus, and we can never take any credit for it.

But God wants all of His children not only to have an eternal home in heaven but also to be awarded the *crown*. It is therefore pleasing to God that we show gratitude *now* by living disciplined, God-honoring lives that will be rewarded. Yes, *rewarded*. Paul could say just before the end that the Lord would "award" him "the crown of righteousness" (2 Tim. 4:8).

The hymn writer Charles Wesley (1707–1788) was moved by Revelation 4:10, when the twenty-four elders "lay their crowns before the throne." Wesley must have been on tiptoes of divine inspiration when he penned these lines:

> Changed from glory into glory,
> Till in heaven we take our place,
> Till we cast our crowns before Thee,
> Lost in wonder, love, and praise![3]

So, to you who say, "I don't care about a crown or prize or reward, I just want to make it to heaven," I ask: How do you think you will feel on that day when you have no crown to cast before the throne? When those around you have the inestimable privilege of taking off the crowns from their heads and laying them before King Jesus, I should think it would be a most horrible, embarrassing, and even shameful feeling to be seen without a crown.

In a word, I want to end well. We all want to end well. In a day when there are more and more shocking revelations of those we esteemed so highly, I urge you to fall on your knees and cry out,

"O Lord, let it not be me." To make sure you are not one of them who is exposed, it will mean following Paul's example: "I beat my body and make it my slave so that after I have preached to others, I myself will not be disqualified for the prize" (1 Cor. 9:27).

Remember, one of the reasons we have the New Testament teaching about rewards at the judgment seat of Christ is so that it will change our lives.

If you, then, are a fallen servant of Christ, taking these words with meekness and a teachable spirit, and following the blueprint for a solid superstructure will enable you to be restored. "You will increase my honor and comfort me once again" (Ps. 71:21).

By the grace God has given me, I laid a foundation as an expert builder, and someone else is building on it. But each one should be careful how he builds. For no one can lay any foundation other than the one already laid, which is Jesus Christ. If any man builds on this foundation using gold, silver, costly stones, wood, hay or straw, his work will be shown for what it is.

—1 CORINTHIANS 3:10–13

My hope is built on nothing less
Than Jesus' blood and righteousness;
I dare not trust the sweetest frame,
But wholly lean on Jesus' name.
On Christ, the solid Rock, I stand;
All other ground is sinking sand.[1]

—EDWARD MOTE (1797–1874)

CHAPTER 3

GOD'S BLUEPRINT

BEFORE WE PROCEED, I MUST ASK YOU A FUNDAMENTAL question: are you sure you are saved? I hope you won't feel insulted at this, assuming you may be a seasoned believer. But the easiest thing in the world is to take for granted what is most important, namely, whether one knows for certain that if he or she were to die today, would they go to heaven?

At Westminster Chapel I introduced Evangelism Explosion (EE), founded by Dr. D. James Kennedy. It is the best soul-winning program I know of. I will never forget that a very mature person, a physician who took EE in London in order to learn how to lead *others* to Christ, realized during this course that she herself had not been truly converted! In other words, she was saved as a result of learning EE!

It is possible that some people who have fallen were not even converted. If you are truly converted, you won't mind reading this chapter. If it should turn out that you have not been saved, it is absolutely crucial that you read every sentence in this chapter. There can hardly be anything worse than building a superstructure on a faulty foundation.

THE FOUNDATION

I must ask you: Do *you* know for sure that if you were to die today, you would go to heaven? If you do not know for sure, read on. If the answer is *yes*, then I must ask another question: If you were to stand before God (and you will), and He were to ask you (which He might do), "Why should I let you into My heaven?" what exactly would you say?

Be honest. Imagine it. You are standing before God, and you must state why you truly believe you should be granted entrance into heaven. What would you say to God? Here are typical answers (I have asked this of thousands of people over the years):

- "I have tried to live a good life."
- "I have done my best."
- "I believe in God."
- "I have been baptized."
- "I was brought up in a Christian home and have been a Christian all my life."
- "I have been sanctified."
- "I go to Holy Communion."
- "I went forward and prayed in a service."
- "I bowed at an altar of prayer."
- "I prayed through."
- "I live by the Golden Rule."
- "I have kept the Ten Commandments."
- "I live by the Sermon on the Mount."
- "I pray to God every day."
- "I have tried to be a good Christian example."
- "I love God."
- "I have tried to be godly."
- "I go to church regularly."

I would have to say that if any of these answers would be what you would say to God, believing that is what qualifies you for getting inside heaven, I have to tell you (with respect) that you are probably not a converted person.

There is basically only *one* answer that shows you are resting solidly on the true foundation: that your reliance for salvation is in Jesus Christ alone—His blood and righteousness. If you know in your heart of hearts that your only hope of getting into heaven is because Jesus Christ *paid your debt on the cross*, you are in good shape! This is because the blood of Jesus, shed on the cross, cried out for justice—and got it! Jesus Christ, who is the God-man, *satisfied God's justice* on your behalf by His shed blood on the cross. Never forget that Jesus was and is God. He was and is God as though He were not man, and yet man as though He were not God. He is fully God and fully man. When *you transfer the trust* you had in your good works *to* what Jesus the God-man did for you on the cross, God declares you righteous in His sight (Rom. 4:5). God declares you *saved*. That is the foundation, the only secure foundation. "For no one can lay any foundation other than the one already laid, which is Jesus Christ" (1 Cor. 3:11).

Are you on that foundation? That is the first question that must be asked. Do you know you are saved? If so, you are qualified to build a superstructure, God's house, on top of that foundation.

One of Paul's favorite phrases to denote that we are on this foundation is "in Christ." He puts these two words together many times. Take a look at how often these two words come together in Paul's epistles—dozens of times. This is because those who have transferred their trust *from* their good words *to* what Jesus did for them (putting all their eggs into one basket) are said to be "in Christ."

Perhaps I have not told you anything you did not already know backward and forward. But do you ever pause to focus on the fact that being *in Christ* implies so much?

Even the non-Christian often has a fairly shrewd idea what the Christian is supposed to be like. But do you sometimes find yourself embarrassingly unlike what you should be? I have to admit that I do. For example, "If anyone is in Christ, he is a new creation; the old has gone, the new has come!" (2 Cor. 5:17). The old has *gone*? What am I to believe when the "old" seems to return? Furthermore, "God raised us up with Christ and seated us with him in the heavenly realms in Christ Jesus" (Eph. 2:6). That being true, how can earthly things possibly matter to me again? I'm sorry, but they sometimes do. Not only that: "He who began a good work in you will carry it on to completion until the day of Christ Jesus" (Phil. 1:6) suggests an inevitably good outcome. And yet some fall after their conversion.

The very same promises quoted above would have been applied to the man in Corinth whose sin was incest (1 Cor. 5:1–5); to Ananias and his wife, Sapphira, who were instantly struck dead for lying to the Holy Spirit (Acts 5:1–10); to Demas, who "loved this world" (2 Tim. 4:10); and to Alexander the metalworker, who did Paul great harm (2 Tim. 4:14).

What went wrong? Some dismiss all the examples in the previous paragraph by saying that they were never converted in the first place. Really? How can they be so sure? How often some of us love to protect our doctrinal biases! Would we have said this about King David immediately after he committed adultery and then ordered Uriah's execution—that his real problem was that he was not a true believer? Or Simon Peter at the time he denied knowing the Lord? It is a fact that, sadly, truly saved people can, and sometimes do, fall.

Not all who make a profession of faith are saved; the parable of the sower makes that clear (Matt. 13:3–23). But the writers of Scripture lead us to assume that the people I mentioned above believed the gospel as much as anybody else who is said to believe. I also know that the best of men are men at best and therefore that the *best* of God's servants—men or women—can fall.

I also know that God can take the fallen and restore them.

THE SUPERSTRUCTURE

When Paul said, "You are God's field, God's building" (1 Cor. 3:9), he used two metaphors—one referring to natural vegetation, the other to that of erecting a material structure. He had just said, "I planted the seed, Apollos watered it, but God made it grow" (1 Cor. 3:6). That is why he said we are "God's field" or "garden" (v. 9, TLB). Paul might have stayed with that metaphor and even given us an exposition of John 15:1–17, which is Jesus's discussion of the vine and the branches. For what Jesus taught about the vine and branches is very like what Paul says about a building in 1 Corinthians 3:9–15.

When Paul switched the metaphor from a garden to that of a building, he used the word *oikodome*, which in this place means two things simultaneously: the *act* of building and the superstructure, that which is *above* a foundation. The act of building is what God does through us, not what He does by Himself without us or what we do without Him. "In this work, we work with God" in order to erect the house He has planned (1 Cor. 3:9, PHILLIPS). God's "building" therefore refers both to the act of building and our erecting the superstructure He has in mind for us.

47

This is what we are—His building, the result of His grace in our lives.

The writer of the Epistle to the Hebrews takes the same line: "And we are his house [*oikos*—a word in the same family as in 1 Corinthians 3:9], if we hold on to our courage and the hope of which we boast" (Heb. 3:6).

In other words, you and I are God's property—His house, His dwelling place, His superstructure, *even His temple*, as Paul will go on to say in 1 Corinthians 3:16–17.

One might therefore hastily assume that if *God* does the building we need not worry, He will do it all! After all, if *God* builds anything it is going to be inevitably flawless and magnificent. But that is not necessarily the case. Even with vegetation there was the cooperative effort between Paul's planting and Apollos's watering; but it was God who made it grow, or "gave the increase" (v. 6, KJV).

You may have heard the story about the meticulous gardener who managed to cultivate and grow the most beautiful garden in the area. Someone said to him, "The Lord has certainly given you a lovely garden."

"Right," said the man. "But you should have seen it when the Lord had it all to Himself!"

This would be the same with God's building, the superstructure. It is therefore both what God does and what we do. Having stated that he laid the foundation, knowing that he had presented sound doctrine to his followers on a silver platter, Paul added these words: "Each one should be careful *how* he builds" (1 Cor. 3:10, emphasis added).

Paul laid the foundation, but he could not build the superstructure for each of his hearers or readers. It is up to *us* to build the superstructure over the foundation. So even though it is called God's building, it is nonetheless what you and I must do by erecting a superstructure upon the foundation. And lest someone misunderstand Paul and think he puts himself as the foundation, he makes sure that we understand: "For no one can lay any foundation other than the one already laid, which is Jesus Christ" (1 Cor. 3:11). In other words, the foundation is Jesus Christ. And those who trust Jesus Christ and the precious blood He shed on the cross are converted and are *in Christ.* To quote again from the aforementioned hymn:

> My hope is built on nothing less
> Than Jesus' blood and righteousness;
> I dare not trust the sweetest frame,
> But wholly lean on Jesus' name.[2]
> —EDWARD MOTE (1797–1874)

All who can sing this hymn and mean every word of these lines in their heart of hearts are saved; this means they are on the foundation and qualified to build a superstructure. Those who cannot sing this and mean every word are still unconverted. This hymn is a good test whether or not a person is truly a Christian. For many people might say the words, but in their hearts they are trusting anything but Jesus's blood— instead trusting their good works, their baptism, their church membership, their gift, their knowledge of the Bible, or even their changed life.

The foundation, then, is Jesus Christ. I must repeat: you cannot build a superstructure unless you are on the foundation.

However, the house of God, which we are, is not perfect. It includes not only all who are saved but also those who are saved and imperfect (which includes you and me). Indeed, "In a large house there are articles not only of gold and silver, but also of wood and clay; some are for noble purposes and some for ignoble. If a man cleanses himself from the latter, he will be an instrument for noble purposes, made holy, useful to the Master and prepared to do any good work" (2 Tim. 2:20–21). That is a very important *if*—"if a man cleanses himself." That is precisely what you and I are required to do. That is what Paul means by being careful *how* we build on the foundation.

It is not a question whether or not you and I are going to build a superstructure; it is a question of *what kind* of superstructure we will build.

CHARACTER VERSUS GIFT

Possibly the most important thing that can be said in this entire book is right here: the quality of the superstructure *pertains to one's character, not one's gifts.* The gold, silver, precious stones, wood, hay, or straw is not a reference to the brilliance of one's gift. A person may be an extraordinary orator, but this would not have anything to do with the quality of one's superstructure. The ability to give a good speech or sermon has a natural explanation. Winston Churchill had a way with words, but this did not mean he was erecting a superstructure of gold, silver, or precious gems when he was prime minister of Great Britain.

So too with the ability to make money, to practice law or medicine, to be a CEO, or to preach well—it proves *nothing* insofar as erecting a solid superstructure. Neither does having the power to thrill an audience, whether by oratory or gifts of the Spirit; or stirring a crowd so that they fall on their faces with the fear of the judgment of God. The gift to do this is not what makes for a good superstructure. If I can extrapolate verses of the Bible with lucidity and simplicity, it is not what will erect a solid superstructure; it is a gift that came regardless of my character. So also with an ability to prophesy, heal, cast out devils, or demonstrate stunning wisdom as Ahithophel apparently had (2 Sam. 16:23). The gift of speaking in tongues, likewise, has nothing to do with building a superstructure.

This is the reason low-profile people or high-profile people can fall. They assume that if their *gift* is functioning under the power of the Spirit of God, they must be right with God. Wrong. For some people the matter of character does not seem to come into their heads. There are preachers who read the Bible not for intimacy with God but only for sermons; if they preach well, they assume their relationship with Christ is good. Wrong again. There are people who have a gift of healing and see people healed under their ministry. They believe that authentic healings validate their ministry and lifestyle. Wrong. There are prophetic people who assume that if they can call out people and tell them things about their personal lives that nobody but the person could know, this prophet must be an awesome man of God. Wrong still again. We have seen that King Saul's prophetic gift functioned after the anointing of God's approval lifted from him (1 Sam. 18:10–12; 19:23).

You may ask, How can gifted preachers, high-powered laymen—CEOs, doctors, lawyers, prophetic people, and church leaders—degenerate to such a level and operate with apparent success but without the approval of God?

I will try to answer that. First of all, this sort of thing crosses not only denominational, vocational, and theological lines but also socioeconomic lines. Proceeding without God's approval often describes the prosperous leader but also the less prosperous. In any case, whatever their background or situation, people like this keep on preaching, praying for people, prophesying, and casting out demons, all the while living double lives without it affecting their ministry or practice negatively (at first). Some of these people, many of them well known, have carried on like this for years and did not get caught. Keep in mind throughout this book that the same applies to both laymen and those in Christian ministry. Some will get exposed; the rest will await God's wrathful judgment on the final Day. I would not want to be in their shoes.

Many of them started well. There was a time when some of these people were totally dedicated to God and His glory—perhaps not all, but some of them. I know what I am talking about—some told me themselves. They not only dedicated themselves to God's glory, but they also *made sacrifices* to get where they were. They left homes and good jobs, resisted sexual temptation again and again, and did not care what people thought; they were prepared to look foolish to the world. They lived without income, slept in cars in parking lots, barely survived with the cheapest of food, and were laughed at by the world. I could go on and on. These people started out in a manner that suggested their names could be added to Hebrews 11, the chapter that describes what people did by faith. The world was not worthy of them.

But something happened. God began to bless them both with followers and, perhaps, finances. More money came in. They did not need to sleep in parking lots. They did not have to eat at McDonald's. Before long some were staying in five-star hotels. Some began to *demand* five-star hotels. They were eating the best food money can buy. Their anointing continued. Then temptations crept in—temptations regarding money as well as sexual temptation. They gave in a bit. They noticed that they still had power the next night at church or the next day at work. They began to covet a greater amount of money. They noticed they could still work efficiently, prophesy, and cast out demons.

They could preach with tremendous effectiveness. Their sinful behavior increased. They could preach as well as ever; people responded as much as ever. Their ability and gifts were intact as much as ever; the anointing they took for granted.

They fell. But almost nobody knew but God Himself. That they did not get exposed made them feel they were *special*, as if they had indemnity, that they were selected by God to do what others could not do. They lied to themselves and concluded that they had God's approval in this—that God knew they had special needs. Perhaps they made the dreadful mistake of equating God's blessing with His approval. Actually, sometimes the opposite is true; we can have times when we are not blessed with the success we pray for but have His approval nonetheless.

At any rate, some of this kind of *success*—numerical and financial—is apparent in the kind of people I am describing today. They continue on as if God is happy and nothing is wrong. Others have gotten caught. Those who don't get caught begin to feel secure; they have managed to carry on for so long they don't worry about getting exposed.

What I am saying in these lines is, unfortunately, the tip of the iceberg. This sort of thing is going on in Charismatic as well as Reformed circles. As I said, sexual and financial scandals cross denominational and theological lines. I know more than I wish I knew about evangelical ministers who have lived double lives for years, and they seem to get away with this.

Some Christian leaders don't get caught because it is, sadly, pornography that has gripped them—sex in secret. When major church conferences and conventions come to town, hotel managers often express surprise that pornography sales do not plummet; rather, preachers seem to watch as much porn as all the other men who visit the hotel. It is a chilling indication that the number one sin among preachers is pornography.

But sometimes pornography does not satisfy, and these people become vulnerable to an actual affair and keep ministering the whole time. This is because, as I keep saying, the gifts and calling of God are irrevocable—without repentance. In other words, God does not bestow or withhold His gifts according to one's character or spiritual life. They are sovereignly given. But God expects us to treat such gifts responsibly and with holy gratitude.

Jesus said that people would claim to do what they do in His very name! "Did we not prophesy in your name, and in your name drive out demons?" (Matt. 7:22). Hiding behind the name of Jesus gives some a false sense of security; they assume "all must be well" if they are doing what they do in the name of Jesus, as if God is going to give such people extraordinary protection.

He won't. He hates the sin more than the hurt He feels when His name is disgraced, and this is why He sends judgment on some, often on His very best, as in the case of King David. If God would expose the only man in the Bible called *a man after His own heart*, why should He not openly judge you or me?

THE LORD BUILDING THE HOUSE

One of my favorite verses is: "Unless the LORD builds the house, its builders labor in vain" (Ps. 127:1). This means that if God is not behind what you are trying to do or build, it will fail no matter how hard you try and how long you work at it.

But the Lord still does not build the house without builders! He builds it, yes, but He uses builders!

Here is what you and I have going for us in building a brilliant and solid superstructure (as described in 1 Corinthians 3): *God is behind what we are wanting to do*—if that means a desire to glorify God. In other words, we are not called to embark upon a project that is speculative or doubtful. A superstructure based on godly character and transparent honesty is inherent in God's blueprint for us. It is what God *wants* for you and me.

God's blueprint is designed to show what is best for us.

For that reason we must take care *how* we build. The reason people fall is that they do not take care to build the kind of superstructure that follows His blueprint.

If any man builds on this foundation using gold, silver, costly stones, wood, hay or straw, his work will be shown for what it is, because the Day will bring it to light. It will be revealed with fire, and the fire will test the quality of each man's work. If what he has built survives, he will receive his reward. If it is burned up, he will suffer loss; he himself will be saved, but only as one escaping through the flames.

—1 Corinthians 3:12–15

There is a broad distinction between character and reputation, for one may be destroyed by slander, while the other can never be harmed, save by its possessor. Reputation is in no man's keeping. You and I cannot determine what other men shall think and say about us. We can only determine what they ought to think of us and say about us.

—J. G. Holland (1819–1881)

If I take care of my character, my reputation will take care of itself.

—D. L. Moody (1837–1899)

CHAPTER 4

THE QUALITY
OF THE
SUPERSTRUCTURE

I N JANUARY OF 1963 I HAD AN UNUSUAL DREAM OF A boa constrictor coming after me. In the dream this large snake was a good distance away. I hoped it would not see me, so I kept low and quiet as well as a good distance away. The next thing I knew it came straight for me and pounced on me. Then I woke up.

A few days later some close friends in Fort Lauderdale, where we were living, invited Louise and me to go hear a faith-healer preacher in a large tent. So many of our friends were mesmerized by this preacher. "RT, you must go and hear him." So we did. On the way into the tent I looked at some books he was selling. One of them was based upon a denial of the deity of Jesus Christ. That, of course, gave me pause before the meeting even started.

We sat in the back, a good distance away from the pulpit. But I already had a funny feeling that my dream of the big snake was about to be fulfilled. The preacher left the platform and called out people way up front. "Have you and I ever met before?" he would ask.

"No," came the reply.

"Do you believe I am a man of God?"

"Yes," would come the reply.

"Do you believe God has told me something about you?"

"Yes," they would say. And, sure enough, he would tell the people things that he could not have known. Everybody seemed to be thrilled.

I whispered to Louise, "He will come back to me shortly."

"Really?" she asked. "Would he come all the way back here?"

"Yes, you will see."

"Here he comes," I said to Louise. He came to the back of the tent, passing up hundreds along the way, and came straight to me for some reason. He stood in front of me and asked me to stand. I did. "Have you and I ever met before?" he asked.

"No," I replied.

"Do you believe I am a man of God?"

"No," I replied as people gasped.

"Sir, have you and I ever met before?"

"No," I said again.

"Do you believe God has told me something about you?"

"No," I said to everyone's astonishment.

He asked a third time, "Are you sure you and I have never met before?" I assured him we had not met. "Do you believe God has told me something about you?"

"No," I said again.

Before I could reach for his microphone to explain why I was so adamantly against him, he took off like a scared rabbit, shouting to the crowd, "Here is a man who is going straight to hell!"

My friends were hurt at my responses. People hissed at me as we walked out of the tent. I felt a little bit odd but knew I had been true to myself. I knew he was a phony.

After we returned from London to the United States in 2002, I learned a few things about this man. He was sought after by the police several times for financial fraud, and he had been refused by many Christian TV stations. Some people fairly close to him suspected that he was promiscuous. Not only that, but today as I write this book, he is back on TV, having found some stations that would take him.

It would be my own view that this man has never been converted. He is an unsaved man who will be like those Jesus described: "'Did we not prophesy in your name, and in your name drive out demons and perform many miracles?' Then I will tell them plainly, 'I never knew you. Away from me, you evildoers!'" (Matt. 7:22–23). Whereas I think some of these high-profile people who have fallen have been truly converted years before, I do not think this particular man was ever saved. My reason for saying this was the kind of Christology he was upholding. A saved man would not propagate such ancient heresy (it was Arianism—the belief that Jesus was God's highest creation but not really God in the flesh).

This is one of the reasons I stressed the gospel and the right foundation in the previous chapter. The man I told about above has never been on the foundation in the first place. People like this somehow manage to get into the church through the *back door*, as it were, like those described in 2 Peter 2:1–3 and Jude 4. This is why we must never take sound theology for granted.

And yet it is possible to be on the foundation, which means you are saved, and also to erect a superstructure made of wood, hay, or straw, which means you will have no reward at the judgment seat of Christ. These are materials that will be burned up on the final Day. The person will be saved, according to Paul, but they will lose their reward (1 Cor. 3:15).

I turn again to you if you have fallen. If you know you are a saved person and that you will go to heaven when you die, the question before you now is, Will you rebuild a superstructure that will bring honor to God?

If you are a fallen man or woman, it is not too late to rebuild. This book has come to you in the gracious providence of God. He would not have given you hope if there were no hope.

The purpose of this chapter is twofold:

1. It will explain what is meant by Paul's metaphors: gold, silver, costly stones, wood, hay, and straw.

2. It will show that your willingness to use the right materials from this point on in your life proves that God has mercifully granted repentance on your part and is evidence that you will be restored and used again.

If you have fallen, it is almost certainly because you did not use the best ingredients to build God's house. I say this because one's fall is not *accidental*; that is, it did not just *happen* all at once but was the consequence of an ill-advised lifestyle. It is what Paul means by building a superstructure out of wood, hay, or straw. The consequences of a faulty superstructure are not only revealed at the judgment seat of Christ; God may call one to give an account in this life in advance of the Judgment.

Remember, we are all building a superstructure. Like it or not, it is not a question of *whether* you or I build a superstructure over the foundation; it is a matter of what *kind of ingre-*

dients we use—gold, silver, and precious stones, or wood, hay, and straw. If you build your superstructure with gold, silver, and precious stones, you will not fall. This is why Peter said, "For if you do these things, you will never fall" (2 Pet. 1:10). By "these things" Peter meant giving diligence to make your calling and election sure by adding to your faith, "goodness; and to goodness, knowledge; and to knowledge, self-control; and to self-control, perseverance; and to perseverance, godliness; and to godliness, brotherly kindness; and to brotherly kindness, love" (2 Pet. 1:5–7).

And yet if you have fallen, you can rebuild, starting now if you have not begun already. If you are willing to do this, it shows a teachable spirit and beautiful evidence that you have a wonderful future. It shows too that you are unlike so many who resented (even rejected) any wisdom offered them after they fell and got caught.

Shortly after Jack Taylor told me of our mutual friend's fall and exposure (see the beginning of chapter 1), I wrote my friend an urgent letter. I pleaded with him, "Don't be like —— [a high-profile person whose immorality was telecast around the world and who became the butt of jokes by TV comedians]." It is well known that the denomination of that fallen TV pastor required that he stay out of the ministry for two years. "No!" he thundered back. "Three months of waiting would be enough punishment!" By refusing to accept his denomination's verdict to stay out of the ministry for that stipulated period of time, this particular individual forfeited a restoration of his old anointing. I'm sorry, but he will almost certainly be forever yesterday's man as a result.

So I pleaded with my friend, "Don't be like ——" Sadly, he resented and rejected my counsel. That was only three years ago. If only he had listened! These three years have gone by so quickly. Many of his other friends warned him as well. Had he truly repented and submitted to those who were willing to help him, he would have been back in ministry today. Our God is a gracious, forgiving God. But he would not listen.

But if you will not be like that and will be willing to build the kind of superstructure that Paul lays down in 1 Corinthians 3:12, you will not only be restored spiritually, but in God's time, you will also be back in a place of usefulness again. What was true of David, Jonah, and Simon Peter—all fallen, forgiven, and restored men—will be true of you as well.

UNDERSTANDING THE METAPHORS— GOLD, SILVER, AND COSTLY STONES

I don't want to press the metaphors too far as to how gold, silver, and costly stones might be applied. But I do know that there are basically three temptations—possibly more so with men than with women—that people face every day and that come under the general headings of *money*, *sex*, and *power*. I am sure there is more to it than that, namely, other things that might bring a person down—alcohol abuse, for example, or a lack of wisdom.

But in this chapter I want to show three things that will build a God-honoring house:

1. Integrity with money
2. Sexual purity
3. Humility

But first, why does Paul use "gold, silver, costly stones" as metaphors for building on the foundation?

Viability. This means what is enduring. Something is viable according to its survival probability. Therefore Paul uses the metaphors of gold, silver, and costly stones because they will survive fire. The point of a solid, lasting superstructure is whether it will survive the fire that will be revealed on the final Day. Wood, hay, and straw will obviously be burned up by the fire. Gold, silver, and gems will not burn. "The world and its desires pass away, but the man who does the will of God lives forever" (1 John 2:17).

Virtue. Virtue means moral excellence. Gold, silver, and costly stones indicate what is truly *good* as opposed to what is artificial, superficial, or counterfeit. The superstructure you and I build must be based on transparent character. In a word, we must be *real.* I know what it is to ask the question of someone, "Is he for real? Is she truly for real?" There are so many counterfeit people around nowadays that when you find someone who is truly genuine, it is a relief and like a breath of fresh air.

Visibility. Whereas the foundation is hidden, the superstructure is visible—a thing to be seen. Gold, silver, and gems are tangible items that you can see. Furthermore, what is more beautiful than a glittering diamond or a genuine ruby or emerald? And what is more lovely than a true, open, holy life? The Christian life is to be lived before the world.

> For me t'was not the truth you taught,
> To you so clear, to me so dim;
> But when you came to me you brought
> A deeper sense of Him.
>
> And from your eyes He beckoned me,
> And from your heart, His love was shed.
> 'Til I lost sight of you,
> And saw the Christ instead.
>
> —AUTHOR UNKNOWN

Variety. Gold, silver, and precious jewels indicate variety. So too with our superstructure. As Christians we are all different. My superstructure will not look like yours, and yours will not look like mine. We all have different personalities, different backgrounds, different struggles, different weaknesses, different strengths, different cultures, and different faces!

Value. Probably the main reason Paul chooses gold, silver, and gems is because they are valuable. There is nothing cheap about gold, silver, or precious stones. Whereas wood, hay, and straw are without value by comparison, God wants our lives to show true *worth.* There is nothing rarer than integrity, honesty, faithfulness, and purity of life.

The question follows, How do we know that our own super-structure is comprised of gold, silver, and precious stones, and not wood, hay, or straw?

I answer, by *application* of good teaching. Teaching must be applied. That means we must put it to practical use. It is not enough to hear and recognize good teaching; it is something we must make work in our lives. I remember going to east London years ago with some friends (who were great *sermon tasters*) to hear a great preacher who had come over from America. After the sermon they said, "Wasn't that marvelous? Wasn't that wonderful?" But I feared immediately that they did not have the slightest intention of applying it to their own personal lives (as was later borne out).

We may get a good feeling when we hear profound teaching or great preaching, or when we sing a hymn or read from the Bible. But that is not enough. We must *do* it as well as hear it. Otherwise we are like the person who "looks at his face in a mirror and, after looking at himself, goes away and immediately forgets what he looks like" (James 1:23–24). It is like Paul's warning, "You, then, who teach others, do you not teach your-self? You who preach against stealing, do you steal? You who say that people should not commit adultery, do you commit adul-tery?" (Rom. 2:21–22).

Take this very book. It is of no value if you do not apply this teaching. If you do not build a superstructure of gold, silver, or gems, it would have been better had you not read this book.

But there is more. You build a good superstructure by how you treat temptation. Oscar Wilde (1854–1900) said, "I can resist anything but temptation." When you give in to tempta-tion you erect a superstructure of wood, hay, or straw. When you resist it you build a superstructure of gold, silver, and costly stones. You may not *feel* like you are building anything. I don't think Joseph *felt* he was doing anything great when he resisted the flirtations of Potiphar's wife. He said *no* to her and probably felt nothing. But the angels said *yes* because Joseph passed an important test in his life. (See Genesis 39.)

The colorful preacher Billy Sunday said that the reason Christians fall into sin so often is because they treat tempta-tion like strawberry shortcake rather than a rattlesnake! "Clothe yourselves with the Lord Jesus Christ, and do not think about how to gratify the desires of the sinful nature" (Rom. 13:14). In other words, the best way to avoid falling into sin is to avoid the temptation. Most of us have a fairly shrewd idea what—and who—will tempt us. If we willingly *walk right into* temptation, we are asking for trouble.

I know a man whose admitted weakness has been pornog-raphy. He has asked me to help him, and I have prayed for him and with him about this. He has since actually gotten the victory over pornography, but part of this victory came when he would require that a television set be removed from his room when he stayed in a hotel. He feared he would not have the strength to resist ordering a pornographic movie, so he would ask that the television set be removed for as long as he was there. I don't think hotel managers get many requests like that! (Hotels make a lot of money through the sale of porno films. In fact, they won't show on your bill that it was particularly a porno film you ordered.) But it was a way my friend proved to himself (and to God) that he was dead serious about getting the victory over pornography. On one occasion when a hotel manager would not remove his television set, he got scissors and cut the plug off. He took the plug to the hotel manager the next day and apologized. "No problem," they assured him. But my friend was truly following Jesus's advice: "If your right eye causes you to sin, gouge it out and throw it away. It is better for you to lose one part of your body than for your whole body to be thrown into hell" (Matt. 5:29).

We build a superstructure that will survive fire by developing the right attitude toward any trial or testing. You cannot avoid trial. In this world you will have "trouble" (John 16:33). But one thing we can do is develop an attitude that will *dignify the trial* when such testing comes.

God usually does not warn us that a trial is coming at such and such a time. If only He would say, when we are in a time of prayer and feeling His presence, "Next Tuesday afternoon, RT, you will notice the sudden withdrawal of My countenance. I will be hiding My face from you." If only! No, it is not like that. It just *happens.* "Truly you are a God who hides himself, O God and Savior of Israel" (Isa. 45:15). No warning, no word from God. He just allows a time of testing to come without notice!

What are we to do? Expect it. Be prepared for it. Stay in an attitude of dignifying the trial rather than panicking and blaming God every time something negative happens. When you complain and grumble during the time of trial, the trial itself is actually doing you no good—plus the fact that you are, at best, building a house made of wood, hay, and straw.

Dignifying the trial, speaking generally, means:

1. Don't panic when sudden testing comes.
2. Don't grumble while it lasts.
3. Do nothing to try to get it over with.

Every trial has its own built-in time limit. All trials end. Some, however, can last a long, long time, as when a person becomes bedridden or housebound from an incurable disease. But generally speaking, any trial that God allows, though we think it will last forever, will eventually end. And when the trial is finally over, the angels in heaven either blush or rejoice based on whether or not we dignified the trial and helped erect a superstructure of gold, silver, and gems.

> Every joy or trial falleth from above,
> Traced upon our dial by the Sun of Love;
> We may trust Him fully all for us to do.
> They who trust Him wholly find Him wholly true.[1]

We build a permanent superstructure, one that will stand the test of fire, by controlling the tongue. I have written a book called *Controlling the Tongue*.[2] It is sobering to know that you and I will "have to give account on the day of judgment for every careless word" spoken (Matt. 12:36), probably my least favorite verse in the Bible!

We develop tongue control by not grumbling during a time of trial, but also by not telling anybody *what they did to us* when you have been hurt by someone. Yes, you may need to pour your heart out for therapeutic reasons, but the main reason we tell what they did to us is because we want to get vengeance and punish those who have hurt us by making them look bad.

Every time you and I resist grumbling, gossiping, defending ourselves, or making ourselves look good, we build a superstructure that will survive the test of fire.

UNDERSTANDING THE METAPHORS— WOOD, HAY, AND STRAW

The wood, hay, and straw of 1 Corinthians 3:12 could refer to eccentric teaching as well as being a bad example of a Christian. For example, many Christians might hold to teaching that is less than biblical, through no fault of their own. It is possible that a sincere Christian could sit under teaching that is not based on sound theology. One is to be forgiven for that, but (happily) this teaching will be burned up at the judgment seat of Christ and will not affect the person's salvation.

However, wood, hay, and straw refer mainly to building a superstructure without the honor of God in mind. Sadly, there are those Christians who are saved because they are on a solid foundation, but their lives sometimes do not show their love for God. They consequently build a superstructure that will not stand the test of fire.

Why does Paul use these metaphors—wood, hay, and straw?

They are *corruptible*, that is, unable to be permanent. Wood, hay, and straw are capable of decay, rot, and becoming useless, unlike gold, silver, and gems. It is not a good Christian who can be so easily lured away from the things of God and become so easily corrupted.

They are *colorless*, unlike gold, silver, and costly stones. Wood, hay, and straw do not make a very attractive superstructure. As

Christians we should have something about us that attracts the world, making them want what we have.

They are *common*. You can find wood, hay, and straw without looking very hard, whereas precious metals and gems are uncommon. The Christian should radiate an aura that is exceedingly rare in the world. It is a sad day when we are so much like the world.

They are *cheap*. Wood, hay, and straw are relatively worthless when compared to gold, silver, and precious stones. The "world was not worthy" of those people described in Hebrews 11 (v. 38) because they were anything but cheap and ordinary. Christians who are like this discredit the faith of Christ and His name.

They are *combustible*. Wood, hay, and straw are easily consumed when set on fire, but the superstructure we are invited to erect, that of gold, silver, and costly gems, can never burn up.

THE FIERY TRIAL

There are two kinds of trials that you and I can anticipate:

1. The fiery trials below (here on Earth). They are bound to come; we are "destined" for them (1 Thess. 3:3). Peter said we should not be surprised over the fiery trial we are suffering (1 Pet. 4:16, KJV).

2. But the ultimate test, the *trial of trials*, will be the fiery trial above when our superstructure will be shown for "what it is, because the Day will bring it to light" by fire (1 Cor. 3:13).

What are the differences between the two trials? Both trials reveal exactly where we are spiritually. The trial below tests our ability to manifest fruits of the Spirit. In the heat of the trial here on Earth there will be an indication whether we are developing true Christian maturity—whether we panic, complain, or dignify the trial. In other words, the heat of the trial below reveals the quality of our superstructure up to that point. It is a fairly good hint as to how we will come through at the ultimate trial—at the judgment seat of Christ.

The trial on the final Day will be the very last test that will ever come to us; it is when the superstructure of wood, hay, and straw will be burned up. After the trial below we can continue to repent and improve, having seen perhaps that we did not do too well. But there will be no chance to improve after the fiery trial above; it will be too late for further repentance.

The fiery trial below and the fiery trial above are alike in that:

1. Both are unexpected, coming without warning.
2. Both expose where we are in our spiritual progress.
3. Both will be a time of great pressure and testing.
4. Both come from God.

These two trials are different in that:

1. The trial below may be hidden from others, but the fiery trial on the final Day will be out in the open. All will see where we are spiritually.

2. The trial below is brought on by earthly pressures through people, persecution, financial troubles, ill health, and so forth, but the trial of the judg-

70

ment seat of Christ will be God's fire without earthly pressures to show our spiritual state.

3. The trial below may come through a satanic attack; the trial above will come entirely by God's intervention of fire and great glory.

4. As we saw earlier, whereas there is opportunity to put things right after a trial here below, it will be too late to improve or be granted repentance on the day of days when the whole superstructure will be tested by God's fire.

The trial below *can* take its shape by God bringing judgment on us. This means being exposed—caught, found out. However painful this must be—and it must be very hard indeed—I can promise you: better now than then. However awful it must be to be judged in the here and now, it will be far, far worse then. This is partly why we have this word: "Why should any *living* man complain when punished for his sins?" (Lam. 3:39, emphasis added). In other words, be thankful for it. It is far easier to receive God's fierce judgment now than on that day. So Paul said, "When we are judged by the Lord [whether through sickness or through premature death], we are being disciplined so that we will not be condemned with the world," which means we will not go to hell (1 Cor. 11:32). Hence at the judgment seat of Christ, if our superstructure is comprised of wood, hay, and straw, at least we will be saved. Our works will be burned up, but we will be saved by fire (1 Cor. 3:15). But it will still be a terrible time for those who have no reward. I don't want that to characterize me.

Therefore the person whose superstructure is burned up will receive no reward. The reward comes to the one who built His house with gold, silver, and precious stones. "If what he has built survives, he will receive his reward" (1 Cor. 3:14).

If you have fallen and have been exposed here below, God has been good to you. Don't complain to Him. Thank Him. One day you will be glad you did. Accept His judgment; it is so you will have another opportunity—not just for restoration and a rebuilding of God's house; God wants to use you again. What is more, this rebuilding of the superstructure means not only more time here below but also indicates that you could receive a great reward at the judgment seat of Christ.

Accept this teaching, and you will show a genuine repentance already. Wait for Him to show the next step forward. In the meantime, I would urge that you fall on your knees, thank God for His righteous judgments, and determine in your heart to rebuild your life along the lines of His blueprint. You cannot do better than that.

Godliness with contentment is great gain.

—1 TIMOTHY 6:6

How then could I do such a wicked thing and sin against God?

—GENESIS 39:9

Young men, be careful about two things in your ministry—money and women; for if there is a scandal related to either of these, God will forgive you, but the people won't.

—R. T. WILLIAMS (1883–1946)

CHAPTER 5

MONEY AND SEX

MOST FALLS AND FAILURES IN THE CHRISTIAN LIFE—certainly with men—can be traced to impropriety with regard to one or more of these three things: money, sex, and power. I will devote the next chapter to power. As I said earlier, I am sure the list is longer than that. A lack of wisdom, for example, can result in one's fall. However, the fear of the Lord is the beginning of wisdom (Prov. 1:7), and when there is the proper fear of God in you, it follows that you will not lack any good thing (Ps. 34:10). "He fulfills the desires of those who fear him; he hears their cry and saves them" (Ps. 145:19).

The fear of God will keep one from doing seriously stupid things, whether it be getting into trouble from a hot temper, feeding on gossip (which saps the spirit), caving in to bad advice, alcohol abuse, being undisciplined when it comes to food, abuse with prescription drugs, missing out on God's will for your life, or embracing serious theological error. In a word, the fear of God is the answer for avoiding these pitfalls.

But at the same time I think that you should make sure you have mastered three particular areas of your life—money, sex, and power, which will require strong personal discipline and self-control. After all, one of the fruits of the Spirit is "self-control" (Gal. 5:23). You will not only be erecting a superstructure of gold, silver, and precious stones, but you also will almost certainly be kept from falling, which comes from building a house made of wood, hay, and straw.

When Paul said that godliness with contentment is "great gain" (1 Tim. 6:6), he might have put this remarkable statement in the context of sex, money, or power. The context is about money, but the truth is that sex, money, and power are so intertwined and related to each other that it is sometimes difficult to discern which ingredient has the weightier influence in one's motivation. Regarding money, Paul wants us to be so content with the privilege of true godliness that eagerness for money is not an intense desire. Regarding sex, he wants us as husbands to love our wives as Christ loved the church (Eph. 5:25–33) so that the pursuit of godliness will remove adultery as a possibility. Regarding power, he wants us to love God and His approval so much that our sole ambition is to have His smile, not the admiration of our peers.

INTEGRITY WITH MONEY

Getting back into ministry after a moral failure requires two things:

1. God's forgiveness and favor
2. People who are willing to forgive and give you a second chance

God's forgiveness is paramount. He can also, if He chooses, give you favor by preparing and opening the hearts of people. But if the people will not forgive and accept you, there is not much you can do about it.

This matter, therefore, goes to show how crucial it is to be absolutely honest and meticulous when it comes to handling money. When it comes to money and sex, I don't think you can be too careful. Living near the edge simply isn't worth it.

A good case can be made that Jesus had more to say about money than any other subject in the Bible. So many of the parables refer to money, so many illustrations. Before the Fall in the Garden of Eden there would not have been a problem with money or financial security. All that one needed was provided without any effort. But after the Fall the man was commanded to work by the "sweat of [his] brow" (Gen. 3:19). Money would not grow on trees.

One reason that Christian people can be so unforgiving with regard to financial scandal in the church is because of their anger that a minister or church leader could deliberately misuse money that was given by people who thought they were giving to God. The willful mishandling of God's money is a serious, serious matter. After all, giving to the church or a Christian ministry is perceived by most Christians as actually giving to *God.* I know that is largely what motivates me to give. I would not want to give money to a cause I thought was not honoring to God; therefore, when I am convinced that a church or Christian organization is governed by integrity and devoted to the glory of God, I want to give all I can to them.

But when I find out that my money, which becomes the Lord's money, was deliberately misused or squandered, I am upset. When people gave to my church (when I was a pastor), or give to my ministry now that I am retired, they expect me to be accountable as to how it is spent.

The love of money is a root of all kinds of evil and, says Paul, "Some people, eager for money, have wandered from the faith and pierced themselves with many griefs" (1 Tim. 6:10). A person can become "eager for money" when that person did not intend at first to get like that. Far from it. What sometimes happens is this. The person starts out in the ministry, whether it be as the pastor of a church or as a minister on TV (or both), full of integrity and zeal for God. But soon that person realizes you need money to pay the bills. He or she begins to express the need for financial help. If on television, that person may say, "Our ministry will not continue without your help." Soon he begins to offer things (books or trinkets) and promise things that will entice viewers to give.

One church leader candidly told me, "People will not give unless you ask for it."

What happens, then, is that the same people who started out with great integrity become preoccupied with staying on the air—or keeping the finances of their church afloat—and they emphasize it more than they ought to. They even begin to say mostly things that they know will ring a bell with viewers. Sometimes theological integrity is compromised. Not that they preach heresy, but they cater to what will *bring in the money*. One prominent TV preacher personally told me that he had to raise "two million dollars every three days." That puts a person under a lot of pressure to keep the money flowing into the post office box.

When one's private lifestyle becomes lavish, and people discover it, an understandable suspicion emerges. People can quickly become disillusioned and stop giving when they find out that their five dollars per month is paying for a multimillion-dollar home. I am not suggesting that there is anything sinful about owning a multimillion-dollar home, but when a ministry would not exist without the sacrificial giving of ordinary people, any financial scandal that emerges causes a lot of anger. We therefore need to be extremely judicious with God's money.

There is a verse in the Bible that says, "Money is the answer for everything" (Eccles. 10:19), speaking pragmatically, and yet some even seize upon that verse and exploit it. And yet, whatever else this startling verse means, it certainly shows that money is not unimportant! But God is the One who can give or withhold mercy when it comes to *anything* (Exod. 33:19). That includes financial blessing. I have thought for a long time that the missing element in the raising of money under the name of God is His sovereignty. The sovereignty of God refers to His right and power to do what He pleases with whomever He chooses. He can bless or withhold blessing. And if I get on television and promise you that "God will bless you and make you rich" if you give to my ministry, I have treated God's sovereignty with contempt (even if I did not mean to).

There are well-meaning preachers around who promise health and wealth and who imply that it is our fault if we do not have both. I would lovingly say to preachers like this: "Don't say, 'God *will* bless you if you give to my ministry,' but say, 'God *may* bless you if you give,' because God can *give* or *withhold* blessing." The truth is, God can give or withhold mercy and be absolutely just either way. But it is so easy to cross over a line when you are under pressure to keep the money flowing in. I don't think God wants *any* of His servants to be under that kind of pressure.

Perhaps the worst kind of financial scandal is promising people a physical healing if they will write in and send for a jar of anointed water as long as they include a gift of a certain amount. There are enough simple and sincere people in the world who fall for this and make the TV preacher rich. I am amazed that God does not smite these preachers rigid. But then I recall how patient God has been with me on other matters, so I lower my voice.

I do wonder if the angels cringe, however, when they hear some TV ministers talk about money and use the promise of prosperity in order to motivate viewers to give to their own ministry. I cannot imagine that God is pleased when we play directly into a person's *greed* (which needs no encouragement to expand) in order to get them to give to one's own ministry.

And yet, as King Saul's gift to prophesy did not immediately lift from him after his being rejected by God, so do some religious leaders somehow apparently manage to bless a lot of people—and, for all I know, see some of them healed—despite their flamboyant lifestyles and lack of integrity. This is partly why we should never presume what is on God's mind regarding a particular ministry, whether it thrives and reaches millions or is not well known.

On the other hand, I anticipate more huge collapses of prominent people in the days that lie ahead. God may wait until the final Judgment to expose most, but I expect to hear any day of Him judging some here below.

By the way, if you want to be restored, I must ask lovingly, would you still want restoration if there were no financial blessing attached?

I offer this advice to anybody who seeks not an earthly empire but aspires to build a superstructure of gold, silver, and gems and who does not want to be exposed by the righteous Judge for abuse of money: *handle money as if there were a live TV camera pointing to you day and night for the whole world to see.* That, my friend, will serve to keep all of us on the straight and narrow. After all, one day all will be out in the open. "For there is nothing hidden that will not be disclosed, and nothing concealed that will not be known or brought out into the open" (Luke 8:17; cf: Luke 12:2; Matt. 10:26). The truth about everything will eventually come out.

PERSONAL FORGIVENESS AND RESTORATION

I must now ask you a hard question—a very hard question indeed: if you knew that God would not use you again, would you still put yourself in a right relationship with Him? In other words, is your only motive—really and truly—to get things right with your Lord Jesus Christ merely because you want to be back in ministry? If so, I fear that is not sufficient. I must admit, I would sympathize with you; I cannot be sure how I would be. So I don't blame you for wanting to get back into ministry. But you must face this question: which means more to you—your relationship with God or your being back in ministry?

Here's another question: would you want to be restored if "being paid" was not also on offer? Would you be willing to do ministry for free?

I don't mean to be unfair, but I would have to question how effective any future ministry would be if that ministry meant more to you—or me—than our having intimacy with God. This could only mean that our relationship with the Father, the Son, and the Holy Spirit would at best be second in our priorities. I'm sorry, but I must say that. If all one wants is to get back to where they once were in ministry and being looked up to in the eyes of their followers, they will fall yet again.

God is their judge, not me. I cannot be sure how I myself would react if I got openly judged for every imprudent thing I have done. But I cannot help but wonder if some of those famous, high-profile preachers worried more over getting caught than they did God Himself. Why could they not have *waited* awhile and submitted to their leaders' wisdom before going back into ministry? It certainly gives the impression that their personal egos meant more to them than what God Himself means to them. I fear they let the *cat out of the bag* as to their true character by rejecting the verdict of those to whom they were accountable. Crocodile tears flowing down one's cheeks after getting caught prove nothing insofar as pointing to whether one is sincere. When a certain friend of mine resented my loving caution, "Please don't be like ——," he sadly gave the impression that he had no real sense of guilt and shame over his fall. It smacked of having little if any desire to get to know God but having only resentment that he got caught. All he really seemed to want was for things to be as they once were.

Although we will examine him in more detail later, I must say here that one of the reasons that God restored and used King David again after his grievous sin and put him back on the throne in Jerusalem was because David accepted his own responsibility and esteemed God's sovereign will above all else. He did not attempt to control his following; quite the opposite. He did not try to hold on to his following or encourage a single person to pursue him into his exile. He even said to Ittai the Gittite, "Why should you come along with us? Go back and stay with King Absalom....May kindness and faithfulness be with you" (2 Sam. 15:19–20). He said to Zadok the priest, "Take the ark of God back into the city. If I find favor in the LORD's eyes, he will bring me back and let me see it and his dwelling place again. But if he says, 'I am not pleased with you,' then I am ready; let him do to me whatever seems good to him" (2 Sam. 15:25–26). When the fallen king was cursed by Shimei, who was pelting stones at him, David refused to respond. Why? "...for the LORD has told him to. It may be that the LORD will see my distress and repay me with good for the cursing I am receiving today" (2 Sam. 16:11–12).

This is a far cry from the way so many fallen heroes have accepted God's judgment upon them. I have seen it all too often. They complain that someone *ratted* on them and resent that person. They defend themselves. They are indignant that they should be exposed. Then, after a while when they have no choice, they accept their lot. But not for long. They want back—*now*.

I will tell you how to recognize the man or woman whom God will use again. It is when they are like King David, as I just described, when they give up trying to hold on to things. It is when they are like Jesus, who "made himself nothing" (Phil. 2:7). Jesus said, "The man who loves his life will lose it, while the man who hates [loves less] his life in this world will keep it for eternal life" (John 12:25). This is the mandate given without exception to every fallen servant of God. Few, however, accept this mandate. But King David did. When I see that kind of spirit of humility that was exhibited by David, I will confidently predict, "There is a man (or woman) God will use again." They might even come back stronger than before.

HANDLING MONEY

As for money, the ability to handle it with godly fear is uncommon. This is why God allows relatively few of His servants to be wealthy. So many who are "eager for money" even wander from the faith (1 Tim. 6:10). Jesus explicitly said that you will "hate the one and love the other" or "be devoted to one and despise the other. You cannot serve both God and Money" (Matt. 6:24). When you realize how Jesus warned of building up treasures on Earth and how dangerous riches are, it is truly appalling that some preachers *appear* to play into people's greed to support their own ministries.

Our mandate is to prize intimacy with the Holy Spirit above financial success. However, to people who esteem a close relationship with God more than they do anything else in the world, there is sometimes granted great financial blessing. Why? It is because such people can be trusted with wealth.

One of the more disquieting things about the *health and wealth* teaching is that, even if it is unintentional, it encourages many people to want financial blessing more than a close walk with God. Most people don't need too much encouragement to seek after financial blessing. They need a *lot* of encouragement to seek after God and godliness. I fear that some welcome the prosperity gospel in order to manipulate God to get what they *want*. I truly fear—I pray I am wrong—that it is not *God Himself* who means uppermost to some of them but financial blessing if they are totally honest. When I listen to some of these preachers (happily not all are like that), I hear very little exhortation to living a godly life to please the Lord but only to get *things* from God. If so, it is *using* God—He is but a stepping-stone to wealth. I don't think God is pleased with this.

It's not that He does not want to bless us financially. He often does. But He wants money to be put in the right perspective.

People need to be taught how to handle money. But they need to be taught most of all that God Himself should be their goal, not the money He may give them.

I grant that God often appeals to our self-interest to secure the obedience He wants of us. "Whoever sows sparingly will also reap sparingly, and whoever sows generously will also reap generously" (2 Cor. 9:6). Bring "all" the tithes into the storehouse, and God will pour out a blessing so great you won't be able to contain it (Mal. 3:10). But when verses like these are quoted over and over and over and over again, one cannot help but wonder if this is all that really matters!

My friend Kenny Samuel, a Church of Scotland minister, told me how hurt he was—and his heart ached—as, listening through the ears of his fellow Scots, he watched one TV minister after another from America. He turned to his wife and said, "If I did not know otherwise, I would think that Christianity is all about money." He was not hearing the gospel. He did not hear that Jesus died on the cross or why He died and was raised. It was one appeal after another to trust God for more "things" here below. It grieved me to hear him say it because I feared he was right.

I hate to think what the end will be for ministries who built their empires almost entirely by appealing to their own *health and wealth* and prosperity teaching in order to get money for their ministries. And yet, ironically and sadly, so much of this money comes from the poorer people of the world. The judgment seat of Christ will reveal exactly what God thinks about this.

Do you want to get rich? If so, be very, very careful.

As I have said, I grew up in Ashland, Kentucky. I well remember a lady in my old church who was extremely poor and whose drunken husband abused her. But she had a glow on her face I will never forget. Her face radiated the glory of God. She was regarded as among the most godly people there. I myself had this impression of her. In my old church people would stand up and give their *testimonies*—especially at the Wednesday night prayer meetings, but sometimes also on Sundays. Her testimony stood out in my memory. She would rejoice with a sense of joy and the presence of God. I can almost see her now, waving her handkerchief. But after I went away to college and returned to Ashland some time later, I noticed what seemed to me to be an abrupt change in her appearance. She now wore the best of clothes and wore exquisite makeup and jewelry, which I assumed she could never afford. What was more, the radiant face was gone. No shine on her face. As for giving her testimony, she didn't give a testimony anymore. I wondered what had happened? The answer came. Her husband had been killed in an accident, and his insurance made her independently wealthy. I was glad for her in a way, but on the other hand I was so sad for her that the money had apparently changed her. This did not need to happen!

Honesty with money comes more easily if money does not mean that much to you. When money means so much to you, the temptation to be less than honest and "sail close to the wind" will be strong; sometimes that temptation would seem too strong. You begin to rationalize, "God knows I need this money at this time, and nobody will know if I use it in a particular way just this once."

Jesus said that those who are faithful in what is least are faithful also in much, referring to money (Luke 16:10). This means that the person who is honest with nickels and dimes will be honest in dollars.

I heard about a businessman, John (not his real name), who was absolutely scrupulous with money. He built his business over the years through hard work and honesty. The time came for him to retire, and he was approached by a wealthy businessman, Bill (not his real name), who wanted to purchase John's company. I knew that Bill did not have the best reputation for honesty, and I was a little worried about John selling his business to Bill. I cautioned John. I was brought into the matter to make sure both sides were happy. But I will never forget what Bill, the wealthier and shrewder businessman of the two, said about the less-experienced John, who had built his company carefully over the years. "John's problem," said Bill, "is that he is a nickel-and-dime man." Bill always wanted to do things in a rather questionable way, overlooking details, not being candid. John wanted every nickel and dime to be accounted for. Bill became very angry with John. John stuck to his guns and won. But John came to realize that Bill's questionable reputation was justified—that Bill was hardly a man of transparent integrity. The honest, *nickel-and-dime* man is a contented man today; Bill is a broken, ill, and sad person. He spends his time in and out of hospitals and hiring lawyers to fend off going to prison.

It is amazing what some people will do for money. The very soldiers who were guarding the tomb of Joseph of Arimathea on Easter morning—the nearest examples to being eyewitnesses to Jesus's resurrection as we are likely to discover—actually took money rather than tell what they knew was true! The chief priests commanded them, "'You are to say, "His disciples came during the night and stole him away while we were asleep." If this report gets to the governor, we will satisfy him and keep you out of trouble.' So the soldiers took the money and did as they were instructed" (Matt. 28:13–15).

Jesus asked an unanswerable question: "What good is it for a man to gain the whole world, yet forfeit his soul?" (Mark 8:36).

I will repeat my advice for anybody reading these lines: handle every dollar and every penny as though a TV camera were monitoring your every move for the world to see. After all, an equivalent of a video replay or DVD will be played for all to see at the judgment seat of Christ. Count on that.

There are some, however, who excuse themselves for handling money in a questionable manner because they are so generous with others. It is like saying, "I may not want everybody to know how I spend, arrange the bookkeeping, and how I may not be totally careful with every penny, *but I do give away a lot of money.* This should make it all right." Really?

If, then, your own fall came through the handling of finances, but you want to be restored, I must lovingly ask, Do you still have the same old love of money and material things? Remember: "For everything in the world—the cravings of sinful man, the lust of his eyes and the boasting of what he has and does—comes not from the Father but from the world" (1 John 2:16).

SEXUAL PURITY

Martin Luther used to say that God uses sex to drive a man to marriage, ambition to drive a man to service, and fear to drive a man to faith. But the irony is, all three of these pursuits need to give way for a nobler motive. For example, *eros* love, physical love, is what God uses to make a man and a woman want to get married, but *eros* is not capable of sustaining a marriage indefinitely. There is another kind of love, *agape* love (unselfish love), which must parallel (not replace) *eros* love if that marriage is to flourish indefinitely. Therefore what God uses to start a process in this case is not what He uses to complete it.

When you and I are commanded to love our wives as Christ loved the church, the verb *agapao* is used. The love that motivated God to send His Son into the world (John 3:16) was *agape*, unselfish love. That is the kind of love you and I are commanded to show to our wives. During the engagement period, or honeymoon, a jubilant husband cannot conceive how he would need a *command* to love his wife. But he finds out sooner or later!

Then comes the challenge. What will sustain a marriage ultimately is not one's physical attraction for each other but their love for God. You show *agape* love to your wife not just because *eros* is at work but also because of your esteem for God's Word. It is your love for God at work. A marriage will succeed when both the husband and wife love Jesus Christ more than they love each other. Your love for God will motivate you to love your wife as Christ loved the church, and you will not commit adultery. *Agape* love is not a feeling; it is an act of the will. You don't pray about whether to show this unselfish love. You just *do it.*

"But my wife will not be submissive to me," says the husband. "She is commanded to submit." (See Ephesians 5:22–24.) Yes. But what if she doesn't? Are you now exempt from obedience to Christ? "I cannot love her as Christ loved the church when she does not submit to me," you may say. And *she* says, "I will submit to my husband when I feel he loves me."

What does one do in this dizzying merry-go-round? There is only one answer: you don't wait for the other to do their duty; *you* must become vulnerable and do what the Lord commands of you.

It is only a matter of time until we face sexual temptation. The sexual urge is physical; it is not merely an emotional, psychological, or ego need. We are all, speaking generally, born with this God-given physical desire. But it must be brought under control or it will lead to the worst kind of grief in this world.

Joseph, the favorite son of Jacob, faced sexual temptation after he was sold by his brothers to the Ishmaelites. Working for an Egyptian officer, Potiphar, Joseph had the opportunity for what might be called the perfect affair. Potiphar's wife began to flirt with Joseph. "Come to bed with me!" she said to him day after day.

"She would not tell her husband; nobody back in Canaan would find out," Joseph might have reasoned. What is more, Joseph might have held a grudge against God for letting all those bad things happen to him.

But Joseph refused Potiphar's wife's overtures. His reason: "How then could I do such a wicked thing and sin against God?" (Gen. 39:9). Most people I know refuse sexual temptation mainly because they fear they might get caught if they give in. But Joseph's reason was that *God would know*. This might have been Joseph's finest hour—when he said *no* to Potiphar's wife. He may have been unaware of any spiritual power within. It may have been extremely hard for him. Perhaps that is why he "*ran* out of the house" (Gen. 39:12, emphasis added). But the angels said *yes*! Joseph passed a most important test during this crucial time of preparation. He did not even know he was in preparation. He could not have known he had been earmarked to be a future prime minister of Egypt. He did not know that all that was going on in his life was the consequence of an Architect's carefully drawn plan. Had he known that God was preparing him for greatness, he might have had further impetus to be honorable. But he did not know this.

That is the odd thing about preparation. It is often an unconscious matter; we don't know that it is *preparation* that is going on. What is happening is this: God is looking down the road for what is coming up and therefore puts things in our path to see how we will react. How we respond will determine the next step forward in God's plan for us. Testing, trial, and even temptation are sooner or later in the package. Not that God directly tempts us. No. But He does *test* us by allowing temptation to come. "When tempted, no one should say, 'God is tempting me.' For God cannot be tempted by evil, nor does he tempt anyone; but each one is tempted when, by his own evil desire, he is dragged away and enticed. Then, after desire has conceived, it gives birth to sin; and sin, when it is full-grown, gives birth to death" (James 1:13–15).

A significant part of preparation, then, often includes the issue of sexual temptation. God does us no favor to let us succeed without passing that test *first*. Dr. Martyn Lloyd-Jones used to say to me, "The worst thing that can happen to a man is to succeed before he is ready." Therefore if a minister reaches what could be called the pinnacle of success and *then* succumbs to sexual temptation, it is tragic indeed. But if the kind of success that brings high profile is delayed until one has mastered his will and manifests the fruit of the Spirit called "self-control" (Gal. 5:23), then he is likely to maintain a high profile and not bring embarrassment to the kingdom.

But suppose you have already fallen? You may say, "It is too late for me." Wrong. If you will prove yourself to be truly humble, nondefensive, and submissive to godly authority, and will be very, very patient, it indicates that God is not finished with you yet.

Maybe *you* have been destined for greatness. I know this much. Sexual temptation is something we all must face, and we must *pass the test* sooner or later if we are going to inherit what God has in mind for us. Until we face temptation and pass this test we will not be fully ready for God's destiny for us.

If you have failed, then, there is still time if true repentance is *granted* to you, or if repentance is a true part of how you honestly feel. Chapter 9 is devoted to this subject of repentance. We will see in more detail there that repentance is "change of mind" (Greek *metanoia*). It is either there or it isn't. If you have to work it up, this is not a good sign. But if you have had a definite change of mind and are sorry, it indicates that repentance has been granted. I choose this word carefully because, as we will see again in chapter 9, repentance is something that God *grants*. God "*granted* even the Gentiles repentance unto life" (Acts 11:18). The Greek word is *edoken* from the verb *didomi*, meaning "it is given; it is a blessed and sovereign gift from God." Notice how Paul uses this word. "Those who oppose him he must gently instruct, in the hope that God will *grant them repentance* leading them to a knowledge of the truth" (2 Tim. 2:25, emphasis added). The worst possible scenario in this connection is to cross over a line whereby God will no longer grant repentance so that you cannot be renewed again unto repentance (Heb. 6:4–6). Therefore when you are able to repent, which means God has given you a "change of mind," fall on your knees and thank Him. It shows that God is still dealing with you.

For some reason, Lot pitched his tent near Sodom (Gen. 13:12), which ominously sends a signal that he was setting himself up for temptation and a fall. The Bible calls him "righteous," however, and he was eventually rescued (2 Pet. 2:7), despite having compromised in a most disgusting way (Gen. 19:8). But he was granted repentance. Jude appears to refer to Lot's rescue by Abraham: "Snatch others from the fire and save them...hating even the clothing stained by corrupted flesh" (Jude 23). This means that, having been delivered from a most terrible folly and granted repentance, we should loathe our past ways so that we disdain any connection with the temptation that we gave in to. "Never again!" we must cry before God, man, and the angels. "Never again!" This is hating the garment spotted by the flesh, which one must do who has fallen and wants to be restored.

I have known some people who have given their testimony about their past life in such a way that I wondered if they were sorry for their new life! Their descriptive references to what they were delivered from smacked of wishing they were still back in it! Hating the garment spotted by the flesh means you are *so sorry* for your folly that you cut yourself off from your past by showing utter contempt for what you did.

You may know the story of Archbishop Thomas Cranmer (1489–1556) who was burned at the stake at Oxford in 1556 for his stand on the Eucharist (the Lord's Supper). He once capitulated to the Roman authorities and signed a confession that he agreed with the Catholic doctrine of transubstantiation. But the truth is, he was very sorry indeed that he signed the confession. In any case, he was ordered to be burned at the stake. Witnesses say that as the flames were encircling his body he deliberately held out the very hand to the flame that had signed the confession and watched it burn first to show his utter sorrow for what he did. That is an illustration of hating the clothing stained by corrupted flesh. This is what Lot must have done after he was rescued. And it is what all of God's fallen servants must do if they expect to be used again.

All I am saying in this section on sexual purity is based upon the biblical premise that the *only* kind of sexual relationship that God commends is within the bonds of marriage between a man and a woman. "Marriage should be honored by all, and the marriage bed kept pure, for God will judge the adulterer and all the sexually immoral" (Heb. 13:4). This means that any sexual activity outside of marriage, whether it be heterosexual or homosexual, is sin. I would define marriage as exclusively heterosexual (sexual relationship between a man and a woman) and monogamous (marriage to one person). But the definition of *marriage* as recognized by British law since 1886 says it best: *the voluntary union for life of one man and one woman to the exclusion of all others.*

This is what the Bible consistently teaches. This has been the teaching of the Christian church for two thousand years. Ask any nontheological, unbiased reader to look up the relevant passages, and they will conclude, "Yes, obviously, the Bible is against sex outside of marriage." The reason I put it like that is that we are now in a generation in which *theologians* sometimes make a case (or try to) that adultery can on occasion be acceptable and therefore not be sinful. It has been called "situation ethics." Therefore what used to be called *sin* becomes legitimized. This has been done also with regard to homosexual practice. This calls to mind the ancient prophetic warning, "Woe to those who call evil good and good evil, who put darkness for light and light for darkness" (Isa. 5:20).

So whether you quote from the Ten Commandments ("You shall not commit adultery" [Exod. 20:14]), or relevant passages on homosexuality ("If a man lies with a man as one lies with a woman, both of them have done what is detestable. They must be put to death; their blood will be on their own heads" [Lev. 20:13; cf. Lev. 18:22]), or the Sermon on the Mount ("I tell you that anyone who looks at a woman lustfully has already committed adultery with her in his heart" [Matt. 5:28]), such passages have stood as the benchmarks for biblical morality. As for homosexual practice, the New Testament is clear on this, too; it is called "perversion" in Romans 1:27 and is forbidden yet again in 1 Corinthians 6:9.

One of the saddest sexual rationales in recent years came out of the affair that President Bill Clinton had with Monica Lewinsky. His playing word games sent a hint to many people, especially teenagers—even teenagers who call themselves Christians. President Clinton insisted, "I did not have sexual relations with that woman, Miss Lewinsky."[1] But the *kind* of sex they had was not regarded by him as "sexual relations"; therefore, many young people today are engaging in oral sex right, left, and center and are saying they are not having "sex."

A prominent evangelical preacher in Great Britain was found to be involved in homosexual affairs. He resigned the ministry and tore up all his sermons. If only he had hated his homosexual practice as much as he despised his ministry! The Reformed world was shocked, as indeed were most Christians in the United Kingdom. Instead of repenting of his sin, he left his wife and three children to engage in homosexual activity, and, it seems, has spent a lot of time *defending* homosexual practice and using the Bible to back it up!

I wrote a book in 1988 called *Is God for the Homosexual?* (answer: yes) in which I sought to demonstrate a love and tenderness toward people who have homosexual tendencies, but at the same time I showed that the practice is sinful.[2] As there are many robust heterosexual Christians who resist temptation day and night rather than grieve God, so should Christian people who are gay in orientation also be required to resist temptation. The gay person's libido is no stronger than that of the heterosexual. But since I wrote that book some twenty years ago, the statistics seem to be changing. More and more people are not only admitting to being gay but this is found among not a few ministers and worship groups, whether Reformed or Charismatic. That also means that Dr. R. T. Williams's warning would be irrelevant for some men today going into the ministry—their temptations are not in the least heterosexual. I fear that the situation is worsening day by day. If this is not the repeat of the days of Lot (see Luke 17:28), indicating the last days, I don't know what is.

And yet Jesus was far more gracious toward sexual sin than He was self-righteous sin. He was far harder on Pharisees for their self-righteousness and pointing the finger than He was the woman found in adultery (John 8:1–11). We must never forget Isaiah's word about Jesus, that "a bruised reed he will not break, and a smoldering wick he will not snuff out" (Matt. 12:20; cf. Isa. 42:1–4). This means that Jesus is extremely tender, compassionate, and forgiving toward those who are sorry and who feel they have no hope but who want somehow to get it right. The *slightest bit of life* and heart cry is enough to attract our Lord's attention. We have a wonderful Savior, one who was tempted at all points, like all of us, but without sin (Heb. 4:15). I pray with all my heart to be more and more like Jesus; that I will not be the slightest bit smug or judgmental toward any fallen servant of Christ, whether it be of a heterosexual or homosexual nature.

Jesus's words in the Sermon on the Mount show that lusting in one's heart is tantamount to adultery. Some sound scholars believe that the Greek should also be understood as *causing one to lust*. In other words, Jesus's words have two meanings:

1. Lusting in one's heart is adultery.
2. "Anyone who *looks at a woman lustfully* has already committed adultery with her in his heart" (Matt. 5:28, emphasis added).

This means that when one *flirts* with a woman with the view of arousing her sexually, even if he does not sleep with her, he has already committed adultery with her in his heart. This flirting could be verbal (as in flattery) or nonverbal (as a facial expression or through a physical touch). When a man does this, even though he has not physically committed the act, he has committed adultery in God's sight. I think too a woman should know that she also is addressed in these lines in the Sermon on the Mount; she should not dress, speak, or touch a man in a manner that is expressly designed to cause him to lust. It works both ways.

As I said, the best way to keep from falling into sin is to avoid the temptation.

No sin brings disgrace upon the name of God like sexual sin. The secular press is thrilled beyond words when a Christian leader falls. They love it. They eat it up. They can't get enough of it. They can't get enough details. They will play it to the hilt hour after hour, day after day, night after night, whether through news or the nighttime comedians. Yes, it is almost entirely for carnal reasons. Not only that; many people (including Christians) are sexually jealous and they love to play "gotcha" with those who fall.

But this does not excuse you or me when we play fast and loose with sexual temptation and when we choose to see how close to the edge we can get without crossing over. I say to you as if on bended knee: *don't be a fool!*

Dr. Clyde Narramore used to say, "Sex was not born in Hollywood but at the throne of grace." Yes. Sex is God's idea, but only in marriage between a man and his wife.

The measure of a man is what he does with power.

PITTACUS (650–569 BC)

You would have no power over me if it were not given
to you from above.

—JOHN 19:11

Man, proud Man,
Drest in a little brief authority…
Plays such fantastic tricks before high heaven
As make the angels weep.[1]

—WILLIAM SHAKESPEARE (1574–1616)

CHAPTER 6

POWER

I STATED IN THE PREVIOUS CHAPTER THAT MOST FALLS in ministry can be traced to a lack of propriety regarding one or more of these three issues: money, sex, or power. It may be surprising at first to see how an impropriety regarding *power* could bring about a leader's downfall. But it comes down to the ancient warning: "Pride goes before destruction, a haughty spirit before a fall" (Prov. 16:18). The near equivalent verse is this: "When pride comes, then comes disgrace, but with humility comes wisdom" (Prov. 11:2). Or take Eliphaz's word to Job that God "catches the wise in their craftiness" (Job 5:13; 1 Cor. 3:19).

When a leader falls from being too ambitious *for* power or too enamored *with* power, it comes about because God caused that leader to trip and be found out. Not all people might recognize that it is God at the bottom of any topple from power, especially if it happens in the secular realm. But that is the way the Christian should perceive a prideful leader's fall. We would not know about King Nebuchadnezzar or King Herod had the accounts of their fall not been recorded in Holy Writ. In the case of King Nebuchadnezzar, he had begun to take himself too seriously. One day he was walking on the roof of the royal palace of Babylon and pontificated, "Is not this the great Babylon I have built as the royal residence, by my mighty power and for the glory of my majesty?" (Dan. 4:30). I suspect the angels said, "Really?" What we do know is that his fall came in moments. However, Nebuchadnezzar was also restored and consequently gave God the glory. He learned his lesson and concluded, "Those who walk in pride he is able to humble" (Dan. 4:37). This is a lesson that all church leaders should know backward and forward.

In the case of King Herod, he gave an address, wearing his royal robes, sitting on his throne before his followers. They shouted, "This is the voice of a god, not of a man." (Acts 12:22). Whereas King Nebuchadnezzar repented and was restored, for some reason God sovereignly stepped in and judged Herod right on the spot. "Immediately, because Herod did not give praise to God, an angel of the Lord struck him down, and he was eaten by worms and died" (Acts 12:23). The ancient word to Moses, "I will have mercy on whom I will have mercy, and I will have compassion on whom I will have compassion" (Exod. 33:19), refers not only to the spiritual realm but to the secular as well.

When John F. Kennedy was asked, "Why do you want to be president?" he answered, "Because that is where the power is."

After Richard Nixon fell, he said he mostly missed the power he had in the White House and the things that went with it. "I could order a helicopter, and it was there in five minutes," he said to a friend. Living in San Clemente, California, after being president was not only humbling for him, but it also left him without power.

When Pontius Pilate was annoyed that Jesus did not answer his questions, he angrily retorted, "Don't you realize I have power either to free you or to crucify you?" But Jesus replied, "You would have no power over me if it were not given to you from above" (John 19:10–11). The Greek word translated "power" here is *exousia*, meaning authority.

God is the sole origin of power, whether it be His creating the universe, the sustaining of creation, derived power (as electricity), political power, intellectual power, financial power, ecclesiastical power, or spiritual power. "No one from the east or the west or from the desert can exalt a man. But it is God who judges: he brings one down, he exalts another" (Ps. 75:6–7). Power belongs to God. When one forgets that, he or she is in a very precarious position.

John Paul Jackson has told of his unusual experience with God—being brought before the throne room in heaven. He witnessed the immediate power of God. For the next three days, he says, he sat on the floor in the middle of a room, crying. He found himself feeling angry with God. He said, having witnessed the infinite power of God in heaven, "Lord, one tiny drop of power from Your little finger put on my hands to pray for the sick would empty every hospital in this town by noon today, but You do nothing about it."

John Paul felt that God gave him this response, "If I gave you the power to do this, I would have to judge you because you are not able to cope with the adulation you would get."

With any measure of power, there will be an equivalent degree of temptation to pride. This is why God promises to exalt those who humble themselves. "For whoever exalts himself will be humbled, and whoever humbles himself will be exalted" (Matt. 23:12). "Humble yourselves, therefore, under God's mighty hand, that he may lift you up in due time" (1 Pet. 5:6). "Though the LORD is on high, he looks upon the lowly, but the proud he knows from afar" (Ps. 138:6).

Therefore when God allows any proud person to get a high profile or attain a respectable level of power, it will follow that:

1. That person will by the Holy Spirit learn humility on the job.
2. That person will be caught out—only to trip and fall.
3. That person will be regarded as a sad, mediocre leader and not admired—even if he keeps his job.

Sometimes it comes soon; sometimes it comes later. But it is only a matter of time. When Dr. Lloyd-Jones said that the worst thing that can happen to a person is to succeed before they are ready, he was primarily thinking of the issues of pride and humility. Not many people can handle overnight success. Sometimes the strength of a person is to be found not in how he or she copes with failure as much as how that person handles success. Or as Pittacus put it, "The measure of a man is what he does with power."

A CALL TO HUMILITY

We saw earlier that Joseph was earmarked for greatness and that he passed the test with regard to sexual temptation. So far, so good. But he would need more than that! Resisting sexual temptation isn't everything. He would have to learn how to *wait* until God's time comes. And during that period of waiting, God has a way of bringing our sinfulness to the surface so that we might confess our sins and turn from them.

The thanks Joseph got for resisting the sexual overtures of Potiphar's wife was a prison sentence. "Thanks a lot, God," he might have said. But when we suffer because we do what is right, we are well on our way to being trusted with success. Yes, sometimes God deals with our faults and failures and secures repentance and improvement in us. We all have had to go through this! "It is better, if it is God's will, to suffer for doing good than for doing evil" (1 Pet. 3:17). "It is commendable if a man bears up under the pain of unjust suffering because he is conscious of God....If you suffer for doing good...this is commendable before God" (1 Pet. 2:19–20).

I heard about a man who was found out for an impropriety and lost his position. He immediately accepted it as God's judgment on him. That was good. But when he talked about it with anybody, he was adamant about how unfair it all was that he was caught as he was and how unjustly his dismissal was carried out. No doubt he had a point. And yet his anger over the way in which it all came about seemed to many to show far more outrage than the indignation he should have felt that he sinned as he did in the first place. If only he had humbled himself under the mighty hand of God and stopped pointing the finger at those who didn't *play fair*, I would have held out enormous hope for him.

Joseph had a lot to forgive.

1. He had to forgive his brothers for their cruel betrayal and selling him to slavery.

2. He had to forgive Jacob for being an unwise father, part of which was showing favoritism to Joseph.

3. He had to forgive Potiphar's wife for her lie.

4. He had to forgive Potiphar for believing his wife and so quickly having Joseph put in prison.

5. He had to forgive the cupbearer to Pharaoh for forgetting to put in a good word for Joseph.

6. He might have had to forgive God—if he was bitter toward Him—for allowing all this to happen to him.

Many of us have had to forgive God. Not that God has ever done anything wrong. He *never* does anything wrong. "He is the Rock, his work is perfect: for all his ways are judgment: a God of truth and without iniquity, just and right is he" (Deut. 32:4, KJV). But we must, nonetheless, forgive Him in the sense that we affirm His *right* to do what He does and honor Him for *permitting* what He does. Forgiving God is continuing to trust Him no matter what and not blaming Him for anything bad that has happened to us, for any injustice or mistreatment He has chosen to allow.

This is one of the lessons Joseph had to learn. As soon as he interpreted the dream of the cupbearer to the king, he could not resist trying to pull strings. Knowing that this royal official would have his job back in three days, Joseph said to him, "Remember me…mention me to Pharaoh and get me out of this prison….I have done nothing to deserve being put in a dungeon" (Gen. 40:14–15). I reckon that his heavenly Father said, "Dear Joseph, I wish you hadn't said that. You are going to need a couple more years."

When Paul said that love is not "self-seeking" (1 Cor. 13:5), I conclude that Joseph had not yet totally forgiven all the above at this stage; otherwise he would not have tried to nudge the arm of Providence as he did. When one totally forgives everybody for all injustice and hurt done to him or her, it produces a rest in God's sovereignty and enables a person to let God be

God and do the exalting in His own time. It is my belief, as I point out in *God Meant It for Good*, that during those two years after interpreting the cupbearer's dream, Joseph came to forgive everybody for all wrongs done to him.[2] This was the final stage in his preparation. Once he was *ready*, God could trust him with success.

I don't mean to be unfair, but if you have fallen and gotten caught but remain bitter toward those who exposed you, you are not ready to return to ministry. And if you are spending your time angling as to how you can return, pulling strings and manipulating the providence of God, it suggests that you are self-seeking and not living in the love described in 1 Corinthians 13.

Humility comes not by seeking humility but by totally forgiving everybody. There are no shortcuts. The essential step you must take if you are going to achieve all that God has envisaged for you—and I am believing that you will come back stronger than before—is to forgive every single person or group you believe mistreated you. If you believe that they lied *about* you, lied *to* you, were unfair, kept you from being vindicated, walked over you, broke their promise to you, have been guilty of the same thing they accused you of, did not give you a chance to explain yourself, betrayed you, or stopped you from getting a second chance because they were determined to block your future usefulness, you have a brilliant opportunity to demonstrate perfect love.

TOTAL FORGIVENESS

I have written two books on forgiveness: *Total Forgiveness* and *How to Forgive Ourselves—Totally*.[3] These two books, summed up, show that you need to forgive others—totally, and you need to forgive yourself—totally.

I will briefly outline what a person must do to be set free. It is *total* forgiveness. This means the following:

1. You must not tell others what someone did to you.

The proof that Joseph totally forgave his brothers was that he made sure that nobody knew what they had done to him (Gen. 45:1–3). It seems that the first thing we do when somebody hurts us is to get on the phone or find someone to tell what they did. Why do we do this? To punish them. Perfect love casts out fear, and fear has to do with punishment (1 John 4:18). Among other things, this means that when we have not forgiven, we want to punish those who hurt us. The chief way we do this is to *tell what they did* to us. We want to make them pay. We cannot bear the thought that anybody admires them. We are determined to get even—to break down their credibility so that nobody will respect them. When we embark in an enterprise like this, it is a dead giveaway we have not forgiven them. We are still bent on vengeance. If you are doing this, you are not ready to be in ministry. I'm sorry, but that is the way it is.

2. You must not let them feel afraid of you or be intimidated by you.

When a person has hurt you, it may give you a gleeful, carnal joy that they are scared of you—that you will somehow hurt them or get even. Can you imagine Jesus being like that to us? Never, never, never allow a person to be afraid of you. This shows your insecurity; it is the mentality of a dictator who keeps his constituency in fear all the time. Joseph did his best to set his brothers free and refused to let them be afraid of him (Gen. 45:4).

3. You must not do anything that would make them feel guilty or angry with themselves that they mistreated you (Gen. 45:5).

Perhaps you want to see the look on their faces when they are proved to have been so awful. You want others to see it. You perhaps fantasize how guilty they will feel one day. Total forgiveness does not require that they admit to their guilt; you forgive them even if they do not think they have done anything wrong. Your model: Jesus (Luke 23:34).

4. You will let them save face.

Instead of "rubbing their noses in it," you cover for them. You completely overlook what they did. You protect their ego and bolster their self-esteem. You say, "They don't deserve to get such treatment." I reply: whoever said they did? Do you deserve graciousness? Nobody does. God lets us save face. Joseph let his brothers save face when he said to them, "It was not you who sent me here [by selling me to the Ishmaelites], but God" (Gen. 45:8). It was perhaps one of the most brilliant demonstrations of total forgiveness in human history.

5. You protect them from their deepest secret and greatest fear.

The eleven brothers' greatest fear was that somehow their father Jacob would find out what they did and what really happened to Joseph. They would rather *die* than for Jacob to learn what they, in fact, did to Joseph. Joseph knew that. It is so moving. Read the account in Genesis 45:9–13 when he tells the brothers exactly what to say to their dad. Joseph writes the script for them; he will not allow them to tell Jacob what they did! So with you. When you protect your enemy from knowledge you could use to destroy them, you are beginning to get free.

6. You must keep forgiving them as long as you live.

Total forgiveness is a *life sentence*. That merely means that you have to keep doing it as long as you live. It is not enough to do it *once*. You must do it today and again tomorrow. And the day after tomorrow. Next week. Next month—every day. Next year—every day. It is a life commitment. You have to keep doing it, especially when the devil reminds you of what they did. Joseph forgave his brothers as long as he lived, even after old Jacob died (when they were so sure Joseph would finally bring vengeance on them). That is when he said to them, "God intended it for good" (Gen. 50:20).

7. You pray for them to be blessed.

When you pray for someone, you do not merely say, "Lord, I commit them to you." That's not good enough at all. You pray that God will *bless* them. "Love your enemies and pray for those who persecute you" (Matt. 5:44). And what if God really does bless them? That is precisely what you prayed for God to do, so don't be upset with Him when He answers your prayer! If you don't mean it, don't say it; but when you can say, "Lord, I ask You please to bless them," you are getting free and fit for ministry.

Joseph was a man devoid of bitterness when he was asked to interpret Pharaoh's dream. This is why he could be trusted with greatness. There is nothing sadder than seeing small, angry men scrambling for power, which they will use for their personal, private platform if they get a chance.

There is a wonderful principle connected to total forgiveness: the greater the suffering, the greater the anointing. If you have more to forgive than others, you have a potential anointing that others do not have. Instead of complaining about "what they did" and giving the reason why you feel you have a right to be angry, you should seize what has happened to you with both hands and totally forgive them, set them free, let them off the hook, and pray that they will be blessed. The result of this will be that you can be trusted with ministry and the possibility of success you never dreamed of. God has done you a singular favor to *withhold* success from you; otherwise it would have destroyed you. But when you have totally forgiven everybody of all they did, you are fit and ready for ministry. It will ensure that God will not let you succeed before you are ready.

THE DESIRE FOR POWER

We have observed that when the apostle Paul said that "godliness with contentment is great gain" (1 Tim. 6:6), he laid down a principle that can apply to sex and power as well as money. What Paul wants for us is that we should love God and His honor so much that we are not inordinately eager for money or driven to look outside of marriage for sexual or ego fulfillment. This therefore means you maintain abstinence if you are single, and, if married, you are content with your wife alone and love her as Christ loved the church (Eph. 5:25ff.), which is the way forward for true godliness and anointing.

First Timothy 6:6 can be applied to the lust for power. The desire for power has set the stage for the downfall for many a servant of Christ. At bottom, the desire for power is craving the honor that comes from people. There is something in so many of us that wants to make people jealous of us. So said the preacher: "And I saw that all labor and all achievement spring from man's envy of his neighbor. This too is meaningless, a chasing after the wind" (Eccles. 4:4). In other words, what drives a person to succeed? It is far too often the thought that people will envy us and be jealous of us; that is what often turns us on. Like it or not, that is the way we are!

I will never forget how this verse (Eccles. 4:4) gripped me one day. It was on April 18, 1988. It convicted me throughout my entire being. I wanted to argue with it and say that this verse may apply to others but not to *me*. But then I was forced to face some questions: why did I choose to do a doctorate at Oxford and not at an American university or seminary? Why did I want a doctorate in the first place? Why do I write books? Why do I have this driving ambition to write yet another? Why did a call to Westminster Chapel mean more to me than a small church in South Florida (which also was on offer)? I could go on and on and on—the list of soul-searching questions is endless.

I was shaken rigid. I felt so ashamed, so embarrassed. Was this truly *me*? Was my motive to succeed largely because I wanted to make people stand in awe of me? I fear that the answer was possibly yes. Not entirely, mind you; for I was doing my best to be led of the Holy Spirit and seek the honor that comes from God only. But Ecclesiastes 4:4 hit me between the eyes as few scriptures have done in my lifetime, and I have sought ever since to be a different kind of man.

This was about twenty years ago. I remember well how I could think of little else for days. I felt as if I was walking around without any clothes on. Was I to believe that my successes (such as they were) would only be explained in terms of my wanting to make people admire me—and have them feel envious?

Oh, of course I could say I did it for God! That would be true, too. But I fear a more carnal motive was too often at the bottom of my pursuits.

But I sought from that day to do something about it, if possible. It has been a quest for God's glory—but only a quest. I still have a long way to go.

Occasionally I get an invitation to return to Ashland, Kentucky, for a high school reunion. I have not been able to attend any of them, but I fear that my motive for going would be quite wrong. I suspect that those who don't turn up (if they are still living) are those who don't have much to be proud of since 1953 and those who do want to be admired.

So much of what drives us to success can also be traced to the desire to please one's parents. I waited a long time before I got my own father's approval. I had wandered from my old teaching as well as my old denomination. I tried hard to compensate. What secured my father's approval more than anything else was that I was occupying the former pulpit of G. Campbell Morgan—one of his heroes.

But the wish for parental approval is not the full explanation. I suspect that the greater driving force to succeed is probably traced to peer relationships—old and contemporary. We want to *show them* what we have done, especially if they were rivals of some sort.

I will refer again to Martin Luther's interesting statement that God uses sex to drive a man to marriage, ambition to drive a man to service, and fear to drive a man to faith.

Yes, God uses ambition to drive a man to service. But the raw, naked wish to make people envious of us must eventually be changed to become an ambition to make God proud of us—not people jealous of us—above all other motives. God uses sex, yes, to drive a person to marriage, and God uses ambition to drive a person to service. But *agape* love and a love for the glory of God must move in or you and I will be anything but content with godliness. We will want more. And that is the recipe for downfall.

TRUE POWER

The best antidote I know for conquering a lust for power is to embrace the implications of John 5:44: "How can you believe if you accept praise from one another, yet make no effort to obtain the praise that comes from the only God?" This question was addressed by Jesus to Jews, revealing precisely why they missed their Messiah. They *made no effort* to obtain the praise of God but were addicted to the praise of men. They preferred the power that they *thought* would give them peace and joy and forfeited the very power that would have truly given such peace and joy.

There are therefore two levels of power: true power and earthly power. True power comes from above—the honor that comes from God only—including the power of the Holy Spirit. Earthly power comes from below: the praise that comes from people.

Therefore when I speak of money, sex, and power, I refer to the transitory, elusive pleasures that come from below. The pleasure that comes from money is temporary; so too the excitement from sexual activity. The adulteress's "house is a highway to the grave, leading down to the chambers of death" (Prov. 7:27). And the power that church leaders too often seek is just as deadly. It is an ego trip that leads away from the power that could have been theirs had they preferred the praise of God to people. Just as the Jews missed the Messiah who was offered to them, so too do many church leaders miss the power that was on offer had they sought God's praise.

The problem is that we suppose that our ambition to succeed is a love for God. Because we believe the Bible and the basic truths of the Christian faith, we tell ourselves that our quest for more influence is for God's glory. This is how we deceive ourselves. We justify our drive to be more successful by saying we can "reach more people," "save more souls," "get our message to the world." Such rationales are nothing but a camouflage for the foolish ego trip we are on.

The truth is that the praise that comes from God would give more power than ever! For one thing, as I just stated, it may include the power of the Holy Spirit. The anointing would open more doors in a day than seeking earthly power would do in a year. But making an effort to obtain the praise of God means seeking the lower seat (Luke 14:7–11), refusing to vindicate ourselves, choosing total forgiveness, and the sheer *waiting* on God's timing. In a word, it is the way of the cross, the life of self-denial, and the participation of the sufferings of Christ.

If you are a fallen servant of Christ but have been granted true repentance—and are gripped by what you are reading in these very lines—God can bring you back to ministry and use you to exceed more than you ever dreamed of. Let no one tell you that you cannot be used again. God would prefer a broken, obedient servant of Christ who has a *past* than an upright, self-righteous Pharisee whose heart is as hard as nails.

But it means self-denial, sexual purity, and the abandonment of earthly power.

Godliness with contentment is great gain. How great? Godliness with contentment can result in power that defies a natural explanation, an anointing that can demonstrate what God can do with one man or woman who is totally resigned to His sovereign will and not bothered by the praise of people.

Finally, Martin Luther said that God uses fear to drive a man to faith. God sometimes gets our attention through fear. Are you afraid? Have you been intimidated by the thought that you are "finished"?

In his great hymn "Amazing Grace," John Newton wrote:

'Twas grace that taught my heart to fear,
And grace my fears relieved.

Yes, that line referred to conversion. But when a backslider returns to the Lord, he or she comes the same old way to the cross. And when you realize that God has truly gotten your attention—and you come humbly with brokenness, truly repentant—you can claim the promise that, when it comes to a bruised reed, which you must be, "a bruised reed he will not break" (Matt. 12:20).

I can remember being almost moved to tears up in the Bodleian Library at Oxford in 1975 when reading the Puritan— "the heavenly doctor"—Richard Sibbes's (1572–1635) sermon, "The Bruised Reed." The thesis of his sermon was summed up in seven words: "Art thou bruised? He calleth for thee." This is because the bruised reed qualifies for God's special love.

Are you bruised? God calls you back. He can use you again.

How the mighty have fallen! Tell it not in Gath.
—2 SAMUEL 1:19–20

In every saint there is something reprehensible.
—JOHN CALVIN (1509–1564)

The best of men are men at best.
—CHARLES HADDON SPURGEON (1834–1892)

CHAPTER 7

THE MIGHTY FALLEN

S OMETIMES IT IS HARD TO FIGURE OUT WHY ONE person is restored after a fall and another isn't. Is it because some sins are worse than others? For example, King Saul disobeyed God by breaking the Law and was not restored; David broke the Law and was restored. As we will see below, Saul broke the ceremonial law; David broke the moral law. And yet David's sin—certainly in some ways—seems worse than Saul's. The sins of adultery and murder seem worse than the wrong person offering a burnt offering. But there was one *big* difference between the two: David truly repented, and Saul didn't.

Jonah disobeyed the word of the Lord to him, but he repented and was restored. And though he was far from perfect, he was mightily used to turn away God's impending judgment upon Nineveh.

Samson let the Lord down most disgracefully but eventually came back and managed to destroy more of Israel's enemies at the end of his life than he did in the whole of it.

This is so encouraging. When there is a genuine, uncontrived, and unfeigned repentance, it shows there is hope—and that God is at work.

But as to why David repented and not Saul and why people like Samson have been granted repentance in the end and others apparently are not remains a mystery. Moreover, why are some found out and others seem to get away with their sin? We will have to wait until the final Judgment for the complete answer. In the meantime I appeal to Paul's glorious submission to the inscrutable and sovereign will of God. "Oh, the depth of the riches of the wisdom and knowledge of God! How unsearchable his judgments, and his paths beyond tracing out! Who has known the mind of the Lord? Or who has been his counselor?" (Rom. 11:33–34). Remaining in awe of this aspect of God's ways should keep us on our knees and make us profoundly thankful when we are given true repentance.

KING SAUL

King Saul's initial fall came from ignoring what the books of Moses had to say about the priesthood and who was qualified to offer the burnt offerings. There are three aspects of the Mosaic Law:

1. The ceremonial law: how the people of Israel were commanded to worship God
2. The civil law: how the people of Israel were to govern themselves
3. The moral law: the Ten Commandments

Only the priests—from the tribe of Levi—were allowed to offer burnt offerings and fellowship offerings (Exod. 32:26–29;

Lev. 6:8–13). Saul came from the tribe of Benjamin and there-fore had no right to do the work of the Levitical priests. But he took advantage of his position as king and presumptuously offered the burnt offerings. Samuel alone was ordained to do this, but he was late in arriving, and Saul became impatient.

"Bring me the burnt offering and the fellowship offerings" (1 Sam. 13:9). No one apparently dared to approach the king and say, "Your majesty, with respect, you are not permitted to do this." Saul not only took the privilege of being king too far, but he also openly went against Scripture.

> "You acted foolishly," Samuel said. "You have not kept the command the LORD your God gave you; if you had, he would have established your kingdom over Israel for all time. But now your kingdom will not endure; the LORD has sought out a man after his own heart and appointed him leader of his people, because you have not kept the LORD's command."
>
> —1 SAMUEL 13:13–14

But Saul was given a second chance, and yet, incredibly, he blew away God's trust a second time! After Samuel told Saul that his kingdom will not endure, Samuel still came to Saul again in 1 Samuel 15:1: "I am the one the LORD sent to anoint you king over his people Israel; so listen now to the message from the LORD." This should have been sweet music to Saul's ears. I would have thought Saul would seize that moment with both hands. God said to him, "Attack the Amalekites and totally destroy everything that belongs to them. Do not spare them; put to death men and women, children and infants, cattle and sheep, camels and donkeys" (1 Sam. 15:3).

God gave Saul a second chance.

What if God were to come to *you* a second time but require an obedience you feel is unfair and unreasonable? As we will see, either Saul did not listen carefully to what God said or he thought he would improve on God's commands! But God sometimes makes a request of us that seems unreasonable at first. God told Abraham to sacrifice Isaac; Abraham obeyed (Gen. 22). This time God was coming to Saul a second time, commanding what Saul seemed to disagree with.

My loving caution to you: if you have fallen—whether you are a *layperson* or a person in Christian ministry of some kind, and God comes to you again, take His word with *both hands*, however unfair or difficult His request seems. He wants to see if you really do want His trust.

But would you believe it—Saul disobeyed! He even justified himself for his disobedience (1 Sam. 15:20–21). Samuel said to him, "Because you have rejected the word of the LORD, he has rejected you as king" (v. 23). That was *it*.

The famous baseball catcher, Yogi Berra of the New York Yankees, used to say, "It ain't over till it's over." But for Saul it was now *over*. The anointing was *gone*.

HEBREWS 6:4–6

In my book *The Anointing: Yesterday, Today, Tomorrow*, I described Saul as a type of "yesterday's man."[1] A most extraordinary thing is that even though the Lord rejected him and even departed from him (1 Sam. 18:12), Saul lived on and held to the kingship for another twenty years. King Saul is an example of one who remains in a high-profile job or ministry but has nonetheless lost the anointing of God's favor. This is amazing. Saul *remained* king although God said to Samuel, "I have *rejected* him as king over Israel" (1 Sam. 16:1, emphasis added). Why did

God let him live? All I know is that God lets some survive even though they cannot ever be renewed again to true repentance.

> It is impossible for those who have once been enlightened, who have tasted the heavenly gift, who have shared in the Holy Spirit, who have tasted the goodness of the word of God and the powers of the coming age, if they fall away [Greek, "having fallen away"], to be brought back to repentance.
>
> —HEBREWS 6:4–6

I am aware that this is a difficult passage. I can safely tell you that I have studied this passage more than any other passage in the Bible. It has been a threat to Calvinists (who teach you cannot fall away) since this verse talks about those who have indeed fallen away. It is a threat to Arminians (who teach that you can be restored after falling away) since this verse says you cannot be brought back to repentance. I believe that this passage refers to people who have truly been saved but are no longer granted the ability to repent of their sins.

Saul was an example of what is described in Hebrews 6:4–6. The writer describes those who fell away but who could not be renewed *again* to repentance. Not that there had been no repentance prior to this. Quite the contrary. When the writer of Hebrews said these people cannot be renewed "again" (Greek *palin* as in KJV) it was because they had been granted repentance before. Indeed, they were enlightened, shared in the Holy Spirit, and tasted the goodness of the Word of God and the powers of the age to come (Heb. 6:4–6). They were truly converted people—as was Saul. For "God changed Saul's heart" and even gave him the gift of prophecy (1 Sam. 10:9–12). But there came a fall—owing to unbelief—for those described in

Hebrews 6 that made it "impossible" for them to be granted repentance after that.

It is a little difficult at first to understand what entails such a fall, especially when you remember that men like Samson, David, and Jonah were renewed to repentance. The answer is that they never ceased to believe God. They persevered in faith and welcomed a second chance. The Greek *parapesontas* ("having fallen away"), even if a conditional warning to the rest of the Hebrew Christians was implied, shows that these people described in Hebrews 6:4–6 had already fallen. This aorist participle comes from *parapipto*. This is a verb from the same family of words also used in Revelation 2:5: "Remember the height from which you have *fallen*! Repent and do the things you did at first. If you do not repent, I will come to you and remove your lampstand from its place" (emphasis added). This shows that the use of *parapipto* or *ekpipto* (as in Revelation 2:5) does not indicate that repentance could not follow such a fall. So what exactly had these people described in Hebrews 6:4–6 done that warranted an inability to be renewed again to repentance?

The answer is unbelief. The result of such unbelief was that they became stone deaf to the Holy Spirit. The context of this sobering passage in Hebrews 6 is Hebrews 5:11. These Hebrew Christians had become "dull of hearing" (KJV). The Greek means that they became spiritually "hard of hearing." The writer had warned of the danger that these Hebrew Christians could *repeat* (rather than repent of) the sin of unbelief, which characterized the ancient Israelites. God said, "I was angry with that generation.... 'Their hearts are always going astray, and they have not known my ways'" (Heb. 3:10). The writer of Hebrews, quoting from Psalm 95:7–8, said: "Today, if you hear his voice, do not harden your hearts." Why did the writer warn these Hebrew Christians in this fashion?

It is because they were already spiritually hard of hearing—but at least they could *hear*! The worst scenario would be what we would call "stone deafness"—that is, to the Holy Spirit. It is when *inwardly* one can no longer hear God speak.

The reason, then, that those described in Hebrews 6:4–6 could not be renewed again to repentance is because they were, spiritually speaking, stone deaf. They could not hear God speak anymore in their hearts. It can happen to a Christian.

This is exactly what happened to King Saul. Inwardly he became stone deaf to the Spirit. Although he wore the crown and remained king for another twenty years, he had no ability to hear God anymore, despite his gift of prophecy being intact for a while.

But why would this irrevocable, tragic, spiritual condition come upon Saul and not David—or Samson? Or Jonah? Was the sin of these Hebrew Christians described in Hebrews 6:4–6 the equivalent of breaking the ceremonial law? Or was it more like breaking the moral law—committing adultery, dishonoring parents, bearing false witness, or committing murder? Possibly. And possibly not. All we know is that they—or at least those described in Hebrews 6:4–6—repeated the sin of ancient Israel who could not enter God's rest (Heb. 3:11, 19).

The answer given, then, as to why ancient Israel could not enter into God's rest was unbelief. This would be the same reason, at bottom, that those described in Hebrews 6:4–6 fell away.

In the case of King Saul, obviously he did not really *believe* what Exodus and Leviticus said about Levitical priests *only* offering the burnt offerings. Obviously Saul did not really *believe* what God said to him about *totally* destroying the Amalekites.

So why did God lift His anointing of approval on Saul and let him carry on as king for another twenty years? The answer is, there is a terminal chastening that does not always end in immediate death. God merely gives one up but lets that person live without any ability to hear Him speak again. This is why they cannot repent; they do not hear God anymore.

Four Kinds of Chastening (Disciplining)

"The Lord disciplines those he loves" (Heb. 12:6). The Greek word for *disciplining* or *chastening* (KJV) means "enforced learning." God has a way of getting our attention—to teach us a lesson. Chastening is not a case of God *getting even* with us for our sins; God's wrath was totally satisfied at the cross! "As far as the east is from the west, so far has he removed our transgressions from us" (Ps. 103:12). Chastening, then, is essentially preparation; it is because God is not finished with us yet. "No discipline seems pleasant at the time, but painful. Later on, however, it produces a harvest of righteousness and peace for those who have been trained by it" (Heb. 12:11).

For many years I have taught that there are three kinds of chastening. But one of my friends who has read this manuscript suggested a fourth—and I treasure this insight. The levels of chastening are:

1. *Internal* chastening

This is when God speaks to us through His Word. That is the best way to have God discipline you—internally, through the Word and the Spirit. If only we would listen!

2. *External* chastening—plan B

It is when we would not listen to Him when He spoke clearly. It is what happened to Jonah; he was found out, and God subsequently sent the fish to swallow him up. Plan B is God making a further effort to get our attention. It is like getting caught. Being exposed. Losing everything. But it isn't "over" yet! There is still hope for the one who experiences plan B.

3. *Secret,* circumstantial chastening

My friend added this chastening. It is a combination of the internal chastening, which is secret, and the external chastening, which is brought on by circumstances. And yet this third type is when a circumstance was used of God to make you quietly come to your senses—something that happens between you and God.

My friend who shared this insight told me this story, which made him feel I needed to add this category. I had recognized him publicly on Sunday evening from my old pulpit as a great leader and example. He was admittedly pleased. But immediately after the service—while still on the premises of Westminster Chapel—he received a phone call that utterly humbled him after getting this public commendation from me. In other words, within one hour of his being publicly praised as a great Christian leader and example, he was inwardly rebuked by something that he felt went against what I had praised him to be. It was not major but enough to keep him from taking himself too seriously. A year or two later when I asked him to sit on the platform when I was to preach at a gathering of the Evangelical Alliance, he refused, saying, "I'd sooner jump off a tower"—having recalled what I have just described. This event in a sense changed his life. Secret, circumstantial chastening. I will have occasion to refer to this again in this book.

4. *Terminal* chastening

Terminal chastening is when it is *over.* Sometimes God brings about death, as in 1 Corinthians 11:30 (those who abused the

Lord's Supper; cf. 1 John 5:16, the sin that leads to premature physical death).

There are two kinds of terminal chastening: that which leads quickly to physical death and that which results in becoming inwardly stone deaf to the Spirit, as we saw in Hebrews 6:4–6—but they live on. The latter was King Saul.

There are probably those in business and professional positions—not to mention the ministry today—with a fairly high profile whose gift functions but who do not hear God anymore. If in business, they continue to make money. If they are professionals, they do their jobs well. If in ministry, like Saul whose prophetic gift functioned for a while (incredible as it may seem), they keep vast followings and supporters behind them.

As for Saul, he irrevocably became yesterday's man even though he wore the crown and had a high profile. I don't want this to happen to you or me.

YESTERDAY'S MAN

We also know *how* he became yesterday's man. If you do not wish to become yesterday's man or woman, there are some things to be considered. In other words, here, summed up, is precisely how Saul became yesterday's man:

1. He put himself above the Word of God.

He knew that a man from the tribe of Benjamin had no right to offer burnt offerings. He knew backward and forward that this was for a person chosen only from the tribe of Levi—and no other. He knew exactly what he was doing when he said, "Bring me the burnt offering." Everybody at the time knew what the Law said about the priesthood and offering the sacrifices. No one would dare do what Saul actually did. But he fancied that since he was king, God made him an exception. Big mistake.

The best recipe I know of how to become yesterday's man or woman is to regard yourself as an exception to the rule. This is one of the devil's favorite ploys in bringing a person down. "God understands your own situation, temperament, weakness, and strengths; He does not expect you to adhere to rules like most people," Satan says. "You are tired; you are very important to God; He would not embarrass you, your family, or allow one to hurt His own name. He knows you have needs that are different from others." The result is, people who listen to the devil put themselves *above* the Word of God rather than *under* it. Sooner or later—surprise, surprise—they fall.

2. He took himself too seriously.

As I said above, he carried the privileges of being a king too far. He assumed he could do Samuel's job.

We must never forget that nobody can do everything. We all have our limits. Saul promoted himself to the level of his incompetence, going *outside* his prescribed anointing. God never promotes us to the level of our incompetence, neither does He lead us to do what we are not called to do. It is our pride—and greed—that takes us outside the limits of our gifting and calling.

It is very humbling to accept the limits of your anointing. You have to come to terms with your own degree of gifting, intelligence, strength, talent, and place. You may want another's anointing, another's job, another's pulpit, another's personality, or another's ability to preach or write. But God made you as you are, and He does not like it when you try to be what you aren't.

A person who takes himself or herself too seriously always wants the credit. Perhaps Saul was even *glad* Samuel was late in coming to offer the burnt and fellowship offerings. It gave him a chance to show that Samuel was not essential to Israel's life and that he too could do what Samuel could do. People like this want all the limelight. They want recognition. Undue significance. Proper respect. Special treatment. They are often among those who succeed before they are ready.

3. He felt *compelled* to do what he did.

Justifying himself for doing Samuel's job, Saul said he "felt compelled to offer the burnt offering" (1 Sam. 13:12). Can you believe it? Compelled?

Imagine that. He felt under some kind of constraint to do what was known to be against the revealed will of God—against Scripture. Have you ever known of someone who said they felt *led* to do what is unbiblical? Have you heard of someone who said, "God told me to do this," even though it is without any scriptural warrant whatsoever?

One of the fastest ways to become yesterday's man or yesterday's woman is to put yourself above the Word of God and then claim that *God* told you to do this.

Here is a good rule of thumb to remember until you die: the same Holy Spirit who wrote the Bible will not lead you contrary to what He already said in His infallible Word. Dr. Martyn Lloyd-Jones used to say that the Bible was not given to replace the miraculous or immediate revelation; it was given to correct abuses. But one thing you can count on is that the Holy Spirit will not contradict His inerrant Word.

If you claim God has told you something when He hasn't, do not be surprised that you can carry on as if nothing happened. He may not strike you dead; He may not even let you get exposed. Instead, He quietly and silently withdraws the anointing of His approval—and allows you to continue as if nothing happened.

4. Saul was accountable to nobody.

He was supposed to be accountable—to Samuel. But he did not listen to Samuel. To whom are you accountable? Do you think you are so close to God and so mature in wisdom and so perfect in your grasp of His will that you don't need the loving counsel and rebuke of a friend? "Faithful are the wounds of a friend" (Prov. 27:6, KJV).

It is safe to say that most people who have a moral failure have this in common: they are not accountable to anybody who will tell them what they need to hear. To be accountable, you have to:

1. Submit to those who know all about you and are unafraid of you.
2. Listen to their rebukes and heed them.
3. Do nothing in secret that they do not know about; do nothing you know they would disapprove of.

We all need someone to whom we will be accountable, those who are not afraid to tell us what we need to hear and who are aware of all our secret activities.

"I'm accountable to God," says the person who is on the brink of a great crash. I have seen it over and over again. Do not be surprised to learn that nearly all those who have a fall also said, "I am accountable only to God."

My friend Jack Taylor and I pleaded with our friend (to whom I referred earlier) when I was still at Westminster Chapel. This man seemed to listen with eagerness to Jack and me as we pleaded with him. We knew nothing—did not even suspect— of any sin in his life. I simply said to him, "You are accountable to no one that we know of. You are supposed to be accountable.

But you're not. And I fear that if you don't listen to Jack and me, you will become yesterday's man."

The news of his fall came three years later.

A well-known church leader has provided the following questions that should be put to each of us regarding accountability:

1. Have you this week been in a situation with a woman that may seem compromising?
2. Have your financial dealings this week been conducted with integrity?
3. Have you exposed yourself to any pornography this past week?
4. Have you spent adequate time in Scripture and prayer?
5. Have you spent priority time with your family?
6. Have you fulfilled the mandates of your calling or vocation?
7. Have you just lied to me?

5. Saul was consumed by jealousy and was threatened by David's anointing.

David killed Goliath and became a hero overnight. The problem was that the women came out from all the towns of Israel to meet King Saul with singing and dancing: "Saul has slain his thousands, and David his tens of thousands" (1 Sam. 18:7).

Oh, dear! What a pity they said that. It was a compliment to David—but not to Saul! Saul took himself too seriously to rejoice in David being complimented. Be careful not to take too seriously the compliments that come to you unexpectedly from out of the blue. They could make you take yourself too seriously, and if jealous people hear about them, they might turn on you. What followed in the case of Saul and David was predictable.

"Saul was very angry; this refrain galled him. 'They have credited David with tens of thousands,' he thought, 'but me with only thousands. What more can he get but the kingdom?' And from that time on Saul kept a jealous eye on David" (1 Sam. 18:8–9).

Jealousy is the easiest thing to see in others and often the hardest to see in ourselves. We all hate to admit to jealousy; it reveals our insecurity, and we don't like to admit to that either.

Beware of your jealous feelings. Pray to God that He will give you objectivity about yourself and cause you to see if what is at the bottom of your feelings is jealousy. It is typical of the sin that precedes one becoming yesterday's man or woman.

6. He lost all sense of integrity.

He stooped so low that he would not even keep an oath to his own son!

What Hebrews 6:18 calls "two unchangeable things," namely, the promise and the oath, refer to two ways God deals with us. A promise is usually presented upon conditions. I will do this *if you will do that.* An oath is stronger than the promise. To swear an oath one swears by a "greater"—in order to be believed. "I swear by my mother's grave," some might say in order to be believed. The oath "puts an end to all argument" (Heb. 6:16). If one swore an oath in ancient times, the one to whom it was sworn absolutely believed it. It was the one time you knew you could trust what was said.

Saul actually swore an oath to his son Jonathan that he would not kill David. Saul even swore by the living God: "As surely as the LORD lives, David will not be put to death" (1 Sam. 19:6). But he broke his word shortly afterward (1 Sam. 19:9–10).

Character is immeasurably more important than gifting. It is our character—integrity—that will matter at the judgment seat of Christ. You and I won't be judged on how well we practiced medicine or law, how much money we made, or how well we preached, wrote, or administered our particular gift. It comes down to one thing: integrity.

7. Saul would apparently repent, and it seemed sincere, but it did not last.

First, he appeared to repent to his son Jonathan. Secondly, he even repented before David. When he realized that David had a perfect opportunity to kill him but didn't, Saul said, "'Is that your voice, David my son?' And he wept aloud. 'You are more righteous than I,' he said. 'You have treated me well, but I have treated you badly.... May the LORD reward you well for the way you treated me today'" (1 Sam. 24:16–19). But Saul continued to try to kill David (1 Sam. 26:1ff.). And yet again, when David could have finished Saul off in one stroke but didn't, Saul said, "I have sinned. Come back, David my son. Because you considered my life precious today, I will not try to harm you again. Surely I have acted like a fool and have erred greatly" (1 Sam. 26:21). It was not a genuine repentance, and David knew Saul would not give up (1 Sam. 27:1).

When Jack Taylor and I pleaded with our friend to come clean and become accountable, he wept like a child. I was so encouraged. But within two weeks, I knew he had not changed after all. When I heard of his downfall three years later, I immediately thought of how Saul would repent, seeming so sincere at the time.

This *repentance*, as seen further in chapter 9, was not the change of mind that God grants to His servants who walk in the light. It is a temporary change of heart that seems real but doesn't last. A person may seem sorry, and you might think he or she has been granted repentance after all, but it may be merely the kind of repentance Judas Iscariot showed when he knew it was too late (Matt. 27:3–4).

8. He sunk to such depths that he participated in the very thing he had condemned.

As king of Israel, Saul had outlawed all mediums and spiritists from the land (1 Sam. 28:9). But at the end of his life he actually consulted the witch of Endor in order to get in touch with the deceased Samuel. It was then that he finally acknowledged what had been true for so long: "God has turned away from me. He no longer answers me, either by prophets or by dreams" (1 Sam. 28:15).

This is what happens to many fallen people—they indulge in the very sin they so loudly condemn.

I am not saying that anybody whose weakness coincides with any of the above examples always becomes yesterday's man or woman.

But these eight propositions should give us pause for thought and could, if we take them seriously, help prevent our walking in the footsteps of King Saul.

More Disappointing Heroes in Scripture

It is encouraging to me that most of God's sovereign vessels have some blemish on their lives. Not all that I will refer to in this section could necessarily be called "fallen." But as John Calvin said in his commentary about Jephthah (Judges 11), "In every saint there is something reprehensible."

Noah

Noah became drunk on one occasion and became extremely vulnerable as a result (Gen. 9:21).

Abraham

Abraham was a man who could tell lies out of fear (Gen. 12:12–13; 20:2), not to mention his unwarranted haste to make good God's promises to him by sleeping with Hagar (Gen. 16:3).

Isaac

Isaac repeated Abraham's pattern of lying (Gen. 26:7) and was deceived by his appetite for a good meal (Gen. 27:4–31).

Jacob

Jacob was the consummate deceiver and manipulator, a horrible father and husband (Gen. 34; 37), and was almost always filled with self-pity, as I show in *How to Forgive Ourselves— Totally*.

Judah

One of Jacob's twelve sons, Judah was exceptionally callous. As Dr. Michael Eaton put it, "It all makes perfectly plain that God's plans go forward by his taking sinners and using them without being put off by their wickedness and brutality."[2] God used Rahab the harlot in one of the most pivotal epochs in Israel's history (Josh. 2; Heb. 11:31). As for Judah, he had been a man with a well-known tendency to immorality and with a harsh, uncompassionate spirit; a man who cared nothing for his brother Joseph or his daughter-in-law Tamar. When Tamar was found to be unexpectedly pregnant, Judah had only one thing to say: Let her be burned (Gen. 38:24). He did not know that he himself was the father. She was widowed and wanted to have children. She pretended to be a prostitute, setting a trap for Judah, and he slept with her. When she became pregnant she proved that Judah was the father (Gen. 38:13–26).

God used this to bring about a great change in Judah's life. It was Judah who pleaded for mercy for his father, Jacob, when the brothers faced the Egyptian prime minister—not knowing it was their brother Joseph. Judah even offered himself as a substitute who would suffer in the place of Benjamin if the prime minister would release Benjamin. Judah was in distress over the thought of further suffering coming upon their elderly father, Jacob. Judah's speech before the prime minister is one of the most eloquent, impassioned examples of intercession in all Holy Writ (Gen. 44:18–34). He reflected the sacrificial love of Jesus in his plea before the prime minister. Judah was a changed man; a sinner became a saint! What is more, all of these happenings in the life of Judah led to God's choice of Judah as the tribe of the Son of David. Of all the tribes of Israel, it was Judah who was chosen to be the royal line leading to our Lord Jesus Christ.

Moses

At the age of forty, when it came into Moses's heart to visit his fellow Israelites, Moses committed murder. If that is not a *fall*, I don't know what is. He grew up knowing he was a Hebrew. Obviously God was dealing with him, and when he could take it no longer, he decided to identify with his fellow Hebrews. He watched them at their hard labor and saw an Egyptian beating a Hebrew. "Glancing this way and that and seeing no one, he killed the Egyptian and hid him in the sand" (Exod. 2:12). But the next day he found out that there were witnesses to what he had done. Stephen says that he thought that his own people would realize that God was using him to rescue them, "but they did not" (Acts 7:25).

The event forced him to flee. All ties with the palace of Pharaoh were severed forever, and Moses was a wanted man. At bottom, however, was his choice to be mistreated along with the people of God "rather than to enjoy the pleasures of sin for a short time. He regarded disgrace for the sake of Christ as of greater value than the treasures of Egypt, because he was looking ahead to his reward" (Heb. 11:25–26).

Moses would have to wait a long time—forty years—before he was used of God. Murder is not exactly the sort of thing one wants on their record. But the fact that Moses was used of God at all—and became the greatest figure of the Old Testament—ought to encourage any person to know that God can use anybody. But you might have to wait a good while before you can be accepted.

Never forget that Moses did not get to enter the Promised Land. God gave Moses an order to "speak" to the rock and water would gush out. He should have known better, but he foolishly *struck* the rock with his rod rather than speak to it as God told him to do. God is no respecter of persons. Moses was severely reprimanded by God and was not allowed to go to Canaan (Num. 20:7–12).

Even the great Moses was human like the rest of us.

Aaron

While Moses was in communion with God on Mount Sinai, Aaron showed himself to be reprehensibly weak. Giving into the people's wicked request, "Come, make us gods who will go before us," Aaron told them to take off their earrings and made them into a gold calf (Exod. 32:1–4). The people "sat down to eat and drink and got up to indulge in revelry" (v. 6). Aaron maintained his place in God's ancient Levitical system but was never trustworthy.

Gideon

Known as one of the great stalwarts of faith (he earned a place in the great "faith chapter" of the Bible—Hebrews 11), Gideon led Israel to victory over their ancient enemies, the Midianites, when all seemed utterly hopeless (Judg. 7). But his life ended under a cloud; he did not end very well. Gideon requested that he be given a share of the plunder from one of the battles, namely gold earrings. The weight of the gold rings came to seventeen hundred shekels. He should have known better, but Gideon made the gold into an ephod, which he placed in Ophrah, his town. "All Israel prostituted themselves by worshiping it there, and it became a snare to Gideon and his family" (Judg. 8: 27). And that is not all. "No sooner had Gideon died than the Israelites again prostituted themselves to the Baals" (Judg. 8:33). It is not a very happy ending or legacy to an illustrious life of a true man of God. In every saint there is something reprehensible.

Jephthah

Neville Chamberlain is remembered in Britain mainly for one thing: his failure as prime minister to recognize Adolf Hitler for who he was. Richard Nixon will be remembered for Watergate and Bill Clinton for his sexual weaknesses. And Jephthah, one of the most powerful men ever to emerge in Israelite history, will always be known for his foolish vow. It eclipsed the victory that won him a place in Hebrews 11:32. He promised God that if he would truly defeat the enemy, Jephthah would give God a human sacrifice—the first person he met at his house. It was a silly, sad, and needless thing to do. But he made a vow—which had to be paid. God gave Jephthah the victory. But the first person he met in his house afterward was his own daughter (Judg. 11:30–40).

Samson

Samson is famous for being the strongest man who ever lived. But it was not a natural strength; it was supernatural—no doubt about that. (See Judges 14:5–20; 15:1–5, 14–15.) But he had a weakness—women. Delilah begged Samson to reveal the secret of his strength. He refused for a while, but in the end she won out, and he told her that his strength was the result of not ever having his hair cut. When he was asleep she cut his hair off. He woke up from the sleep, unaware that his anointing left him. Indeed, one of the scariest and most sobering lines in the Old Testament are these: "But he did not know that the LORD had left him" (Judg. 16:20). This shows how our anointing can be taken away without us feeling a thing. And when Samson tried to do what he had always been able to do previously, he was weak as a child. The Philistines took advantage of Samson's pitiful state. They seized him, gouged out his eyes, and took him to Gaza. The future seemed hopeless. But his hair began to grow, and at the very end of his life, he was given his old anointing and "killed many more when he died than while he lived" (Judg. 16:30).

It is my hope, although it is very faint as I write these lines, that the man Jack Taylor and I have remonstrated with will still be a Samson. I literally pray for this every day. If God could restore a Samson, even though it was done under tragic conditions, he could restore anybody.

Eli

Dr. Lloyd-Jones and I used to talk about Eli, a man who hardly earned a place in Hebrews 11. "But I always thought there was something authentic about him," Dr. Lloyd-Jones used to say. "I felt sorry for him." A powerful priest in his day, Eli took young Samuel under his wings. It was to his credit that he recognized that God was dealing powerfully and unmistakably with the boy Samuel (1 Sam. 3). Eli's awful blemish on his life was that he allowed his wicked sons to carry on without doing anything about it. He knew how his sons desecrated the sacrifices and how they slept with the women who served at the entrance to the Tent of Meeting. He gave them a slap on the wrist—but little more (1 Sam. 2:22–25). It was God's will to "put them to death" (v. 25); they died in battle (1 Sam. 4:11). It was not so much when he heard that his sons were killed in battle that jolted Eli but when he heard that "the ark of God has been captured." Immediately he fell off his chair and died (1 Sam. 4:17–18). Despite his weaknesses, he somehow maintained a respect for the ark, and this is what seemed to matter most to him in the end.

Hezekiah

A king of Judah at the age of twenty-five, Hezekiah "did what was right in the eyes of the LORD, just as his father David had done" (2 Chron. 29:2). He got rid of idolatry in Israel, purified the temple, and celebrated Passover as it had not been done in years (2 Chron. 30:26). "There was no one like him among all the kings of Judah, either before him or after him" (2 Kings 18:5). Hezekiah did "what was good and right and faithful before the LORD his God. In everything that he undertook in the service of God's temple and in obedience to the law and the commands, he sought his God and worked wholeheartedly" (2 Chron. 31:20–21). But there came a time when his heart was "proud and he did not respond to the kindness [of God] shown him" (2 Chron. 32:25). But Hezekiah repented of his pride. He saw a wonderful deliverance from the threat of Sennacherib, king of Assyria, and God also extended Hezekiah's life by fifteen years (2 Kings 20). All this points to a king who truly loved God.

But I have always had a sinking, uneasy feeling with the way Hezekiah's life ended. He unwisely showed the king of Babylon everything in his palace, whereupon Isaiah prophesied that everything in his palace would be carried off to Babylon, and, "Some of your descendants, your own flesh and blood who will be born to you, will be taken away" (Isa. 39:7). That to me is a pretty awful thing to look forward to. But Hezekiah's reaction to this? "'The word of the LORD you have spoken is good,' Hezekiah replied. For he thought, 'There will be peace and security in my lifetime'" (Isa. 39:8). It is written that "God left him to test him and to know everything that was in his heart" (2 Chron. 32:31). Though he loved God, what was also in his heart was pride and selfishness.

Jonah

Given a commission to go to Nineveh, God said, "Go," and Jonah said, "No." Then God said, "Really?" Jonah opted for a Mediterranean holiday—Tarshish (Spain). The Lord sent a wind that was so violent it got all the sailors' attention. They cast lots to see who on the ship caused this. God overruled, and Jonah was found out. "Throw me overboard," he told them, for he knew he was the reason for the storm. They did. A great fish swallowed Jonah (Jon. 1). I love the way the King James Version begins Jonah 2:1: "*Then* Jonah prayed" (emphasis added)! He prayed as he never prayed in his life. What did he pray? He asked to do the very thing he had refused to do!

What will it take to make you pray? How much do you pray? Children spell *love* T-I-M-E. What if that is the way God spells your love for Him? How much *time* do you spend in prayer? Listen to these words from Martin Luther's journal: "I have a very busy day today. I must not spend two, but three, hours in prayer." John Wesley would not think of going out into his day without two hours on his knees. But there aren't many Luthers or Wesleys around. As a matter of interest, perhaps you should know that the average church leader in America and Britain spends *four minutes a day* in prayer or quiet time. And we wonder why the church is powerless!

There is an old saying that says, "God doesn't compel us against our will, but makes us willing to go." The fish worked. Jonah repented, pleaded, cried, and promised. At the bottom of all this, God was mercifully at work. God did not have to send the wind, but He did. He did not have to overrule the rolling of the dice of the sailors, but He did. He did not have to send a fish to swallow Jonah, but He did. And He did not have to give Jonah a second chance, but He did.

"Then the word of the LORD came to Jonah a second time: 'Go to the great city of Nineveh and proclaim to it the message I give you'" (Jon. 3:1). Jonah obeyed this time.

Here is my opinion: had Jonah not obeyed when God came the second time, he could have been given what I have called *terminal chastening*. In other words, alongside His external chastening—plan B—he was also given a second chance. But had he rebelled after the second chance, I suspect he could have been in the worst scenario. God may have taken his life. Or Jonah might have lived, but had he said no yet again, I believe that Jonah would have been in a Hebrews 6:4–6 situation—unable to be renewed unto repentance. I would not press this too far; it is my opinion. Neither do I know what goes on in God's mind or a person's heart that warrants judgment so that they cannot be used again. For all I know, God may have given Jonah a third, fourth, and fifth chance. I know how patient He has been with me! So I would not want to press my point of view on this too far.

But when one hears God's voice say, "Go," it shows they are not stone deaf to the Spirit. One should take *any* clear word from God with both hands. Seize the moment!

Jonah was given a second chance. He obeyed. Not that he was perfect! He was angry that his message was not vindicated. He preached that in forty days Nineveh would be overturned (Jon. 3:4). He looked forward to seeing the destruction. But the people repented, and God did not send the calamity Jonah promised. Jonah sulked and pouted. But God was very patient with him (Jon. 4).

Therefore God gave a disobedient man a second chance. And, as I said, we find out that he was still less than perfect when you read the account (Jon. 4). I have asked, did Jonah ever learn his lesson? I think he did. After all, in telling the story, he let God have the last word (Jon. 4:11).

That is the key. Let God have the last word. If God could use Jonah after his disobedience and repentance, He can use you or me.

Have mercy on me, O God,
   according to your unfailing love;
according to your great compassion
   blot out my transgressions.
Wash away all my iniquity
   and cleanse me from my sin....
Cleanse me with hyssop, and I will be clean;
   wash me, and I will be whiter than snow....
Restore to me the joy of your salvation....
Then I will teach transgressors your ways,
   and sinners will turn back to you.
                    —PSALM 51:1–2, 7, 12–13

I've wandered far away from God,
Now I'm coming home;
The paths of sin too long I've trod,
Lord, I'm coming home.[1]
            —WILLIAM J. KIRKPATRICK (1838–1921)

CHAPTER 8

THE RETURNING BACKSLIDER

THE TITLE OF THIS CHAPTER IS BORROWED FROM THE great Puritan Richard Sibbes (1577–1635), known in his day as "the heavenly doctor." Dr. Martyn Lloyd-Jones used to talk about how two of Richard Sibbes's sermons helped him when he was feeling extremely tired and discouraged many years before: "The Bruised Reed" and "The Returning Backslider." The former is of immense encouragement to one who feels very weak in their faith; the latter was written mainly to encourage those who have fallen and to show them how willing God is to receive one back. Either of these sermons are sweet for those who want to sense the tenderness of God toward one who is feeling low. I want that same spirit of graciousness to govern all I say to you. If I come through as hard and inflexible—and moralizing—I will have failed. I sometimes think that if you moralize people, you can also demoralize them.

The word *backslide* means "to relapse into error or bad ways." The word *backslider* or *backsliding* is used only in the Old Testament, mostly in the King James Version. "The backslider in heart shall be filled with his own ways" (Prov. 14:14, KJV). Because it is not specifically used in the New Testament, one can almost "manufacture" its meaning. For example, does it refer to a truly converted person who falls into sin? Yes, in my opinion. Or could you call one a backslider who merely makes a profession of faith but goes back into the world? I think not, in my view, although some would call anybody a backslider who made a profession who does not persevere. I do not believe that all who make a profession of faith are truly saved; therefore I would rather not use the term *backslider* for all who make a profession of faith but only those who have come to saving faith in Christ.

Backsliding is a word used by Jeremiah and Hosea. "Your backsliding will rebuke you" (Jer. 2:19). The NIV generally prefers the word *faithless* (Jer. 3:6, 8, 11–12, 14), "turned away" (Jer. 8:5), "unfaithful" (Jer. 31:22; 49:4), although it translates, "Return, faithless people; I will cure you of backsliding" in Jeremiah 3:22 and "Our backsliding is great" in Jeremiah 14:7. But at the same time, God declared He is "married" to the backslider (KJV), "for I am your husband" (Jer. 3:14). Hosea promised, "I will heal their waywardness" (Hos. 14:4, "backsliding"—KJV).

On a scale of one to ten, all of us have been backsliders to some degree. If *one* refers to nonscandalous sins (hurt feelings, not praying enough, lethargy) and *ten* to scandalous sins (the blatant abuse of money, sex, and power), who among us has not been in a backslidden state, at least at the lower end of the scale, at some point in our pilgrimage? Although Peter does not appear to be addressing "backsliders," there is that intriguing comment, "For you were like sheep going astray, but now you have returned to the Shepherd and Overseer of your souls" (1 Pet. 2:25). For every sin, however great or small, is a turning away from God. After all, "All have sinned and fall short of the glory of God" (Rom. 3:23). Coming short of God's glory is not merely a preconversion activity, for, "If we claim to be without sin, we deceive ourselves and the truth is not in us" (1 John 1:8). One of my favorite hymns ("Come, Thou Fount of Every Blessing") includes this verse:

> O to grace how great a debtor
> Daily I'm constrained to be!
> Let Thy goodness, like a fetter,
> Bind my wandering heart to Thee.
> Prone to wander, Lord, I feel it,
> Prone to leave the God I love;
> Here's my heart, O take and seal it,
> Seal it for Thy courts above.
> —ROBERT ROBINSON (1735–1790), PUBLIC DOMAIN

Although the word *backsliding* is not found in the New Testament, the parable of the prodigal son (Luke 15) surely shows, among other things, that a true child of God can get off the rails and then come back to the Lord. Our heavenly Father loves to welcome the backslider home. We must never forget too that the older brother in this parable was indignant when the prodigal got so much attention. I don't mean to be unfair, but a returning backslider can anticipate some older brothers in the church who will not be too welcoming!

Many people have been told that a fallen pastor cannot be restored. A friend of mine who had a moral failure sought help from a book on this subject, reading it almost in desperation. He was hoping for a word of encouragement that he could be used again. What he read gave him no hope. It might have demoralized him. I cannot imagine that an inflexible approach that gives no hope for future usefulness to fallen Christians— ministers or laymen, high profile or unknown—could be in the Spirit of Jesus.

The truth is, God can use *anybody* who has truly repented. He can open doors that would normally be closed, break down barriers that would normally preclude usefulness again, and open people's hearts that had been cold and prejudiced. To the fallen person I say: Your task is to repent fully; God's job is forgiving, restoring, and opening doors. It dignifies the blood Jesus shed on the cross that a fallen saint could be forgiven and be used again.

I know a lot more than I can reveal in this book. I know of people who have fallen and repented and have come back stronger than before. I know of others who have fallen and repented and have not attained to former heights. I only know that God is not limited should He choose to make the latter house "greater than the glory of the former" (Hag. 2:9). We limit Him by our defensiveness and lack of true repentance.

I know of divorced people who have remarried and have been used of God in a most extraordinary way. Some of them have a high profile. I think too of old Dr. W. M. Tidwell, who came to my church in Ashland, Kentucky, at the age of eighty, and whose impact on me as a teenager was most profound. I recall that there were those who would never accept him because he had been divorced and remarried when he was young. When I think of the hard line taken by certain ministers as I grew up— not to mention some today—I am all the more amazed to see the variety of people God uses. Louise and I will celebrate our fiftieth wedding anniversary in 2008, and I am so indebted to God for the way He has blessed us. To those who have not been as fortunate, I say: God gives fresh beginnings. When Jesus said "every" sin (KJV—"all manner of sin")—other than blasphemy against the Holy Spirit—shall be forgiven, this includes divorce (Matt. 12:31). God hates divorce (Mal. 2:16), but divorce is pardonable.

There is also such a thing as theological backsliding. This kind of waywardness does not get as much attention as those sins that relate to money, sex, and power. But this too needs to be addressed. The Galatians had backslidden theologically and spiritually. They had been influenced by Judaizers (Jews who professed faith in Christ and required that the Law, including circumcision, be imposed on Gentiles) and imbibed much of their teaching about the Law. When Paul said, "You have fallen away from grace" (Gal. 5:4), he was rebuking them for opting for a gospel of works rather than grace alone and trying to win them back. We won't know until we get to heaven whether they came back to the teaching of Paul. But he was mainly referring to their doctrinal waywardness, not to their moral conduct. However, one would have to say that theological backsliding is rooted in a spiritual condition. A person can outwardly keep the Ten Commandments and be spiritually bankrupt.

My point is this. Sometimes a person—layman or preacher—gets off the rails doctrinally and needs to be cautioned, if not slapped hard on the wrist. But if they lapse into sheer heresy, they should not be allowed to teach, preach, or be involved in ministry until they have repented of their error and have been sorted out.

KING DAVID

The only person who is described in the Bible as a man after God's own heart (1 Sam. 13:14) had what is arguably the worst fall of any child of God described in Scripture. And yet I doubt that anybody, certainly among all the kings of Israel, loved God more than David. The psalms are replete with words that demonstrate an intense, unwavering love for the Most High God.

I will praise the LORD, who counsels me;
    even at night my heart instructs me.
I have set the LORD always before me.
    Because he is at my right hand,
    I will not be shaken.

—PSALM 16:7–8

Though you probe my heart and examine me at night,
    though you test me, you will find nothing;
    I have resolved that my mouth will not sin....
Keep me as the apple of your eye....
And I—in righteousness I will see your face;
    when I awake, I will be satisfied with seeing your
    likeness.

—PSALM 17:3, 8, 15

The LORD has dealt with me according to my
    righteousness;
    according to the cleanness of my hands he has
    rewarded me.
For I have kept the ways of the LORD;
    I have not done evil by turning from my God.

—PSALM 18:20–21

May the words of my mouth and the meditation of my
    heart
    be pleasing in your sight,
    O LORD, my Rock and my Redeemer.

—PSALM 19:14

Search me, O God, and know my heart;
    test me and know my anxious thoughts.
See if there is any offensive way in me,
    and lead me in the way everlasting.

—PSALM 139:23–24

I have quoted what is merely the tip of the iceberg from some of David's psalms. He had a deep, deep love for God but equally a great, great fear of displeasing God—unlike anybody else I can find in the Old Testament. "O LORD, do not rebuke me in your anger or discipline me in your wrath" (Ps. 6:1). "I know that you are pleased with me, for my enemy does not triumph over me" (Ps. 41:11). "Teach me your way, O LORD, and I will walk in your truth; give me an undivided heart, that I may fear your name" (Ps. 86:11).

God had been singularly good to David. He was a shepherd, chosen "from the sheep pens" (Ps. 78:70), a man most unlikely to be a future king of Israel. God raised him up to kill Goliath. David became an overnight hero. That is, until the women sang, "Saul has slain his thousands, and David his tens of thousands" (1 Sam. 18:7). Killing Goliath was in a sense the best thing that ever happened to young David, but it must be said also that it was the worst thing to happen to David. David's overnight success was evaporated by his becoming—also overnight—the most wanted and hunted man in Israel.

God spared David from Saul. He also spared David from killing Nabal, the churlish and small-minded husband of Abigail. Moments before David was going to get vengeance upon Nabal, Abigail interceded and kept David from doing something he would have regretted for the rest of his life. He said to her, "May you be blessed for your good judgment and for keeping me from bloodshed this day and from avenging myself with my own hands" (1 Sam. 25:33).

When we realize how God *kept* David from getting vengeance upon Nabal and how David so consistently controlled himself, behaving himself wisely in all the days of King Saul, who was determined to kill David (1 Sam. 24:4ff.; 26:8–11), we may ask, "Why didn't God stop David from folly later on?" You tell me.

I only know that God made David king over Judah (2 Sam. 2:4), then king over Israel (2 Sam. 5:3). He conquered Jerusalem, something that no human being had ever done before (2 Sam. 6). He defeated the Philistines right, left, and center (1 Sam. 5:20). He brought the ark to Jerusalem (2 Sam. 6:17). It was as if he could do nothing wrong. He seemed invincible.

But one day he got up from an afternoon nap and saw a very beautiful woman bathing. Her name was Bathsheba. He found out that she was married—to one of his own soldiers. What David thought would be a one-night affair ended in a melancholy surprise—she became pregnant. This was not the news David wanted. "No problem," he seemed to say. David sent for Bathsheba's husband, Uriah the Hittite, to come home for the weekend that he might sleep with his wife and cover the adultery and identity of the real father.

It didn't work. Uriah had what Puritans might call an "overly scrupulous conscience." He could not bear the thought of sleeping with his wife while his fellow soldiers were at war. Uriah refused to sleep with Bathsheba, no matter how hard David tried to make it happen.

The man after God's own heart, who stated how pleased God had been with him, not only became an adulterer but also a murderer. David instructed his general Joab to put Uriah at the hottest part of the battle so he would be killed.

It worked. Uriah was slain. David seemed to get away with it.

And he did for about two years. I have often wondered whatever was on David's mind during those two years. Did he write any psalms? He might have. It is amazing how one's anointing can flourish regardless of one's behavior. Never forget that the gifts and calling of God are "without repentance" (KJV) and "irrevocable" (Rom. 11:29). In other words, David's not repenting of his sin would not have stopped his anointing from working. I do not know that David wrote any psalms during this time. I am saying that he might have. We will find out when we get to heaven.

But it was not until the prophet Nathan came to David that there was any repentance. This was the same Nathan who at first gave David permission to build the temple, then had to return to David and admit that both of them had jumped the gun. Nathan and David had mutual respect for each other. But David was not prepared for what Nathan was about to uncover. He perhaps underestimated the depth of revelation a true prophet can have.

Some of the most haunting and sobering words in the Old Testament are these: "But the thing David had done [namely, his adultery, cover-up, and murder] displeased the LORD" (2 Sam. 11:27).

God might have overruled and stopped David from committing adultery. He might also have not allowed Bathsheba to get pregnant. He might have allowed Uriah to sleep with Bathsheba to cover up David's paternal identity. But David ended up a murderer as well.

It is also possible that, had David truly repented immediately after his adultery and murder—with a broken and contrite heart—God might graciously have forgiven him and let David get on with his life without bringing Nathan back into his life. You may recall the third kind of chastening mentioned earlier: *secret*, circumstantial chastening. What if David had been brought to his senses before Nathan came to him? I would certainly not try to prove this, but in my pastoral experience I have known of those who sinned, then repented—and were spared public exposure. I would only say to you, if you have fallen but have been spared the public exposure, fall on your knees before God, confess your sin, and turn from it—utterly and totally—and ask God for mercy that your sin does not become public knowledge. Who knows? If you are truly a changed man or woman, without further disciplining, God may spare you of the hurt and embarrassment and sorrow you so much dread. This could be a way the aforementioned third level of chastening—*secret, circumstantial*—might be applied.

But God let the worst scenario happen in David's case. Remember, dear friend, if God would allow the worst possible situation to emerge with a man after His own heart, He may well allow it with you or me.

Nathan began his confrontation with King David with a parable. The gist was this: A wealthy man stole the only ewe from a poor man, then slaughtered the lamb for a special guest. David burned with anger. "As surely as the LORD lives, the man who did this deserves to die! He must pay for that lamb four times over, because he did such a thing and had no pity!" (2 Sam. 12:5–6). Isn't it noteworthy how self-righteous and judgmental a sinner can be! We saw the same thing with Judah.

Sometimes we who have our weaknesses can pontificate loudly and eloquently to the people out there, moralizing them—when we possibly have a greater problem than anybody we preach to!

"You are the man!" Nathan had to say to David. Nathan revealed to David how good God had been to David *and* how much had been revealed to Nathan. "I anointed you king over Israel, and I delivered you from the hand of Saul. I gave your master's house to you, and your master's wives into your arms. I gave you the house of Israel and Judah. And if all this had been too little, I would have given you even more. Why did you despise the word of the LORD by doing what is evil in his eyes? You struck down Uriah the Hittite with the sword and took his wife to be your own" (vv. 7–9).

There was good news and bad news. The good news: God forgave David. The reason for this: David was not defensive. He did not deny it. He did not make excuses. He did not blame anybody. He took the total responsibility and never looked back. "I have sinned against the LORD," he immediately stated (v. 13).

Nathan replied, "The LORD has taken away your sin. You are not going to die" (v. 13). This was very wonderful news. This meant that, unlike King Saul, who was not granted repentance nor was he ever renewed to unfeigned repentance for the rest of his life, David was different. He was truly sorry. He prayed:

> Have mercy on me, O God,
>   according to your unfailing love;
> according to your great compassion
>   blot out my transgressions.
> Wash away all my iniquity
>   and cleanse me from my sin.
>
> For I know my transgressions,
>   and my sin is always before me.
> Against you, you only, have I sinned
>   and done what is evil in your sight,
> so that you are proved right when you speak
>   and justified when you judge.
>   —PSALM 51:1–4

The good news, then, is that David was not only found out but forgiven. Very good news indeed.

The bad news: Nathan prophesied to David, "The sword will never depart from your house, because you despised me and took the wife of Uriah the Hittite to be your own.... Out of your own household I am going to bring calamity upon you. Before your very eyes I will take your wives and give them to one who is close to you, and he will lie with your wives in broad daylight. You did it in secret, but I will do this thing in broad daylight before all Israel" (2 Sam. 12:10–12).

God is no respecter of persons. The man after God's own heart would be severely chastened and disciplined. What would follow for the next several years was sadness and tragedy—all coming from within David's own family.

When I was at Westminster Chapel, I preached for two years on the life of David. But when I came to the end of 2 Samuel 11, I lost heart. I announced to the deacons that I was ending the series on David. It happened to be about Christmastime, and I would be changing the sermons anyway for a couple of weeks. However, I did not intend to return to the life of David. "Why?" they asked. I replied that I did not have the *stomach* for it—all that was left in the life of David, beginning with 2 Samuel 12 was so discouraging. I simply did not want to preach on what I called the *downside of David*. They accepted my verdict.

But after Christmas, during the first week of January, our church had a whole day of prayer and fasting. I was not prepared for what happened to me on that day. It was as though the Lord Himself came into our living room and had a conversation with me. It went something like this: "So you aren't going to preach anymore on the life of David?"

"No," I replied.

"Don't you know that what you are calling the *downside* of David *is where most of your people are?*"

I was stunned. I announced to the deacons the following Sunday night what I felt I had learned on our day of prayer and fasting—and that I would continue in the life of David. These men were thrilled. I can tell you, the following six months or so turned out to be the most exciting part of the whole series. These sermons are now in my book *A Man After God's Own Heart.*[2]

I do not claim to have a prophetic gift. Rarely, if I am honest, do I feel that God gives me a word for someone. But He did this, I believe, with respect to a fallen brother whom I know well. I told him that he would have a future ministry, but it would be like the *downside* of the life of David. He may never attain to his former heights and glory. But God would use him. He broke down and wept in gratitude. It has turned out in that precise way. He does not have the following, the support, or the success of his previous days, but God is using him.

All that Nathan prophesied came true. Too true. Literally true. First, the child born to Bathsheba died. Second, his son Amnon raped his sister Tamar—who confessed this to her full brother Absalom. When David heard of this, he was "furious" (2 Sam. 13:21) but did nothing. Absalom waited two years and then killed his brother Amnon. Absalom fled to avoid the wrath of his father, King David. But eventually he returned to Jerusalem and was reunited with his father. If only that were the end of the story.

Absalom made a decision to conspire against his father, the king. He engineered a high profile before all the people at the city gate and secured a vast following. If David knew about this, he would have probably assumed that Absalom was doing a lot of good stuff—if only to show how glad he was to be back in his father's favor. But he did things that subtly undermined confidence in the king. He assured them that if the king would not give them justice, Absalom certainly would be there for them. It would seem that the king took the loyalty of his people for granted; he did not apparently feel a need to maintain a close touch with them. David had no idea that Absalom would do such a thing.

But he did. "He stole the hearts of the men of Israel" (2 Sam. 15:6). In a most underhanded way, Absalom asked David for permission to worship the Lord in Hebron. Permission was granted. Then Absalom sent secret messengers throughout the tribes of Israel to say, "As soon as you hear the sound of the trumpets, then say, 'Absalom is king in Hebron'" (2 Sam. 15:10). All went according to Absalom's plan—and according to Nathan's awesome prophecy.

The bottom line: David was forced to flee from Jerusalem.

Preaching through the *downside* of David's life convinced me many years ago that any reward David will receive in heaven will be based not only on his years prior to the events up to 2 Samuel 11, but also on those heartbreaking episodes described from 2 Samuel 12–24. In other words, David will not receive a reward in heaven because he killed Goliath or became Israel's greatest king; it will be because he rebuilt a superstructure in 2 Samuel 12–24 that would become the basis for a reward in heaven. His attitude after his downfall is what revealed the real character of David as a man.

David knew instantly that all Absalom did was part of God's judgment on him. He never fought it, not for a moment. He submitted to it. He did not call his following to rise up and resist Absalom. He did not try to hold on to what was rightly his—the kingship, the palace, the people of Israel as a whole.

It is here that we see a further reason that David was a man after God's own heart. He knew he had greatly grieved the Lord. He knew that God himself was behind all that was going on. He took Absalom's conspiracy with utter dignity and grace.

In a word, he did not despise the chastening of the Lord. (See Hebrews 12:5–11.) But do not forget, God's chastening, or disciplining, is not His getting even with us. As I said, God got even at the cross (Ps. 103:12). Chastening is essentially *preparation*. God goes to great pains to discipline us because He is preparing us for what is ahead. Chastening comes because God is not finished with us yet.

God was not finished with David. But David had no way of knowing what God might be up to. He did not fight God's judgment.

I would say lovingly to you—if you have known the chastening of the Lord, it's not for nothing. Whom the Lord *loves* He chastens (Heb. 12:6).

You will say: Did not God chasten Saul? Yes. And God gave Saul a second chance, and Saul blew it.

You will say: But Saul was not a man after God's own heart.

I reply: The way to find out whether *you* are a man or woman after God's own heart is to *submit totally* to God's judgment. Do not deny what you did. Do not be defensive. Do not make excuses. Do not blame this person or that. Admit it; confess it; submit to what God is doing.

Let the *downside of David* be your blueprint and model. Do what David did.

What did David do?

1. *He did not resist God's judgment.*

"Come! We must flee, or none of us will escape from Absalom" (2 Sam. 15:14). The king set out with his entire household following him.

2. *He did not try to amass a greater following.*

When Ittai the Gittite showed up to follow David, the king tried to discourage him. "Go back and stay with King Absalom" (2 Sam. 15:19).

3. *He accepted what was apparently the new regime.*

Note: He calls his son King Absalom! He had no idea whether he would be back in Jerusalem—ever again.

4. *He refused to take the ark of God with him.*

Zadok the priest, who was determined to stay with David, had brought the hallowed ark, symbolizing the presence of God, from Jerusalem. "Take the ark of God back into the city," David ordered (2 Sam. 15:25).

5. *He utterly submitted to the total sovereignty of God regarding his future.*

"If I find favor in the LORD's eyes, he will bring me back and let me see it [the ark] and his dwelling place again. But if he says, 'I am not pleased with you,' then I am ready; let him do to me whatever seems good to him" (2 Sam. 15:25–26). David knew that God said to Moses, "I will have mercy on whom I will have mercy, and I will have compassion on whom I will have compassion" (Exod. 33:19). He knew that there was nothing he could do to manipulate the sovereign will of God. He simply bowed to it.

This is what you and I must do. I have asked myself the question, writing these lines: What if I myself were in this very situation and found myself under the gracious but severe judgment of God? Would I react as David did? Would I? Would you? *Will* you—if this is the situation you are in as you read these lines? Will you say, "Let Him do to me whatever seems good to Him"?

To put it another way, David unwittingly followed the advice of Paul:

> Your attitude should be the same as that of Christ Jesus:
> Who, being in very nature God,
>   did not consider equality with God something to be
>   grasped,
> but made himself nothing,
>   taking the very nature of a servant.
> —PHILIPPIANS 2:5–7

Jesus did not hold on to the glory He had in heaven before the Word was made flesh. We too are told to be that way, not holding on to what is so precious to us. David did not try to hold on to his kingship. He let it go. He knew God was at work. As he put it when the evil man Shimei cursed David—and David did nothing in return, "Leave him alone; let him curse, for the LORD has told him to. It may be that the LORD will see my distress and repay me with good for the cursing I am receiving today" (2 Sam. 16:11–12).

These were hard, hard days for David. As he continued up the Mount of Olives, he did so "weeping as he went; his head was covered and he was barefoot. All the people with him covered their heads too and were weeping as they went up" (2 Sam. 15:30). When we sin against God, others are affected by it too. These people probably did not know that all that was happening was rooted in God's displeasure with David's sinful act. David knew. He was weeping for one reason, they for another. He was weeping because of his folly and the fallout of his sin; they were weeping because they loved King David.

But there was one faint rainbow that could be traced through the rain: the power of prayer.

6. *David prayed.*

Whereas he did not lift his smallest finger to defend his kingship, there was one thing he could engage in that was entirely legitimate: prayer. That is something we all can do. We turn to God and make our requests—then wait and watch Him work.

David had suddenly received new information that disquieted him perhaps more than anything yet. "Ahithophel is among the conspirators with Absalom" (2 Sam. 15:31). Losing the support of Ahithophel was devastating news. Although he was not regarded as a prophet, Ahithophel certainly had the gift of wisdom. As far as we can tell, he never got it wrong. "In those days the advice Ahithophel gave was like that of one who inquires of God. That was how both David and Absalom regarded all of Ahithophel's advice" (2 Sam. 16:23). Ahithophel was like Dr. Henry Kissinger to President Ronald Reagan. When Absalom won Ahithophel over to his side, it was a major coup. David knew the implications of this news. What could he do?

One thing, then, was left for David: he prayed. "O LORD, turn Ahithophel's counsel into foolishness" (2 Sam. 15:31). I don't know how much faith David really had when he uttered that prayer. It was asking for the impossible. But that was all David could do.

7. *David acted shrewdly when God gave an earnest of answered prayer.*

After praying as he had done, Hushai the Arkite unexpectedly showed up to support David. David seized the moment. He told

Hushai that he would be a burden if he followed David around but suggested that he return to Jerusalem: "You can help me by frustrating Ahithophel's advice" (2 Sam. 15:34). That is exactly what Hushai did. Ahithophel's advice would have ensured the throne for Absalom. (See 2 Samuel 17:1–4.) Ahithophel's plan was accepted, but Absalom himself suggested that they summon Hushai, "So we can hear what he has to say" (2 Sam. 17:5).

This was the turning point. Hushai replied to Absalom, "The advice Ahithophel has given is not good this time," whereupon Hushai gave counsel that was carefully designed ultimately to hand the throne back to David. Lo and behold, Absalom and all the men said that the advice of Hushai was better! "For the LORD had determined to frustrate the good advice of Ahithophel in order to bring disaster on Absalom" (2 Sam. 17:7, 14).

God answered David's prayer.

David's exile was temporary. David eventually returned to Jerusalem as king. At some point, David wrote Psalm 51, which includes these words:

> Cleanse me with hyssop, and I will be clean;
> > wash me, and I will be whiter than snow.
> Let me hear joy and gladness;
> > let the bones you have crushed rejoice.
> Hide your face from my sins
> > and blot out all my iniquity.
>
> Create in me a pure heart, O God,
> > and renew a steadfast spirit within me.
> Do not cast me from your presence
> > or take your Holy Spirit from me.
> Restore to me the joy of your salvation
> > and grant me a willing spirit, to sustain me.

> Then I will teach transgressors your ways,
>> and sinners will turn back to you.
>
> —Psalm 51:7–13

The reference to *hyssop* refers to the blood of a sacrifice. Hyssop was used to sprinkle the blood (Exod. 12:22). Any returning backslider is in need of the blood of Jesus as much as when he or she first came to the Lord.

One of the most important statements in Psalm 51, however, is these words: "The sacrifices of God are a broken spirit; a broken and contrite heart, O God, you will not despise" (v. 17). This is the key—a broken and contrite heart. This is the reason David could be used again. As we saw, there was brokenness from the first moment Nathan showed David his sin. No defensiveness. No excuses. No blaming others.

What David did in committing adultery and trying to cover it up was pretty awful. I don't think it gets much worse than that. So he was found out and also forgiven—and restored.

If God could do that with David, He can do it with you too.

Then Judas, which had betrayed him, when he saw that he was condemned, repented himself, and brought again the thirty pieces of silver to the chief priests and elders, saying, I have sinned in that I have betrayed the innocent blood.

—MATTHEW 27:3–4, KJV

Then Peter remembered the word Jesus had spoken: "Before the rooster crows, you will disown me three times." And he went outside and wept bitterly.

—MATTHEW 26:75

There are two kinds of repentance: one is that of Judas, the other that of Peter; the one is ice broken, the other ice melted. Repentance unto life will be repentance in the life.

—WILLIAM NEVINS (1797–1835)

CHAPTER 9

REPENTANCE

THE PURPOSE OF THIS CHAPTER IS TO GO MUCH deeper in pursuing the meaning of repentance. We are dealing with a word that is far more complex than many suppose. For one thing, as we will see, there are no fewer than three Greek words used in the New Testament that could be translated "repentance."

This chapter is extremely important for three reasons. First, as I stated above, according to a good number of counselors and Christian psychologists, there is too often a pattern among those who have repented of their failure, namely, that they return to the same sin that brought their downfall—after three to five years. They were doing so well for a good while. But they slipped back. I wish this were not true. I certainly do not want this to be true of you. We must therefore do what we can to ensure that this does not happen to you.

Second, it is essential that you know you have been renewed to the kind of repentance that shows you have not become stone deaf to the Holy Spirit. You need to know you are *not* like those described in Hebrews 6:4–6, which we examined above. In other words, as long as we can hear God's voice and be renewed to repentance, we are not irretrievably yesterday's men or women. When there is unfeigned repentance because you hear the voice of the Holy Spirit, there is glorious hope.

Third, when we have fallen and want to be forgiven and used again, there is more needed than the repentance that is a part of saving faith. This is why we must examine the Greek in some detail.

The key to restoration is true and continued repentance. But there are levels of repentance. And when one has grievously fallen after having believed and having been in any kind of public service or ministry, it is essential that the deepest level of repentance characterizes the person who wants to be restored. Let there be no arrogant snapping of the finger to God as if to say, "OK, Lord, I'm sorry—now give my previous usefulness back to me," expecting God to stand at attention as if to salute you.

My first pastor as I grew up in Ashland, Kentucky, was Dr. Gene Phillips. His influence on me was profound. He had unusual power in the pulpit but also extraordinary charisma with people on a one-to-one basis. This may have had a slightly negative fallout, however. I remember so well a man in my old church—Marvin. His spiritual state seemed tied to Gene Phillips. When Dr. Phillips moved from Ashland to another city, Marvin stopped coming to church and apparently went back into the world. But when Dr. Phillips was invited to return to Ashland to preach, Marvin would be on the front row—and was the first to go to the altar after the sermon. But his "repentance" lasted only a few days. I remember too when we heard Dr. Phillips was coming back to Ashland yet again to preach, we all said, "Marvin will be back in church this Sunday." Yes, there he was—on the front row. It wasn't Dr. Phillips's fault, but I do wonder whether Marvin was ever truly converted.

On my first trip to Israel in 1969 we stayed in a hotel on the Palestinian side of Jerusalem. A very colorful Arab—called Samir—sold beads and trinkets to the people day by day as we would leave the hotel for the bus, and he would be waiting for us when the bus returned to the hotel later in the day. With a very pleasant smile, Samir would shout out, "Beads? Do you want to buy some beads? Jesus saves! Jesus is coming soon! Hallelujah! Do you want to buy some beads?" We knew he had picked up a bit of the "language of Zion" after so many Christian tourists had come in and out of the area.

On the following Sunday at the Baptist church near the Old City of Jerusalem, my friend Dr. Jess Moody preached. It was an unforgettable morning. Jess preached a wonderful sermon. And when Jess gave his appeal for people to come forward and receive Christ, who would come forward but Samir? We were all thrilled. Jess could already envision telling his people back home how he led a Palestinian to the Lord while in Israel. But our hearts sank when, as it turned out, Samir was first outside the door as we were leaving the church. He shouted out, "Want to buy some beads? Jesus saves! Jesus is coming soon! Hallelujah! Want to buy some beads? Jesus saves!"

Samir had a motive for walking forward in that Baptist church. He knew more of these people would buy beads from him rather than others who had their trinkets to sell too. I suppose he had done this many times before. There was not the slightest thought of his acknowledging that Jesus died on the cross or believing in his heart that Jesus rose from the dead—much less was there any change of mind—which is what repentance is.

There has been a type of preaching, especially among some fundamentalist churches in America, that might lead a person to believe that if he or she walks forward in front of the people after the sermon when the "altar call" is given, sign a card that Jesus is his Savior and Lord, and be baptized, that person has been converted. I'm sorry, but this sort of thing has happened to tens of thousands. True repentance—a change of mind and turning from sin—sometimes does not enter the picture at all. This is not true of all such churches, of course. Neither is it true of all who respond to a preacher's appeal, but it is true of too many.

We must now deal with a theological question: which comes first in the *ordo salutis* (order of salvation)—repentance or faith? I answer: it depends on how you define *repentance*. If repentance is defined as "turning from every known sin," as some Puritans put it—and that this is a prerequisite to be saved—many people would never know whether or not they were saved because they would always fear they had not repented enough! It would be an endless bondage. This is why, as we saw earlier, so many sincere believers have lacked assurance of their salvation. But if repentance means a *change of mind*, as we will see below, then it does not matter which comes first—faith or repentance.

If, however, you are a fallen Christian—whether minister, layman, leader, or follower—and want to be used again, I do not think that coming *back* to the Lord is quite the same thing as coming to Him the first time. In other words, when you come initially to Christ in faith, you are trusting wholly and only in the blood He shed to wash away your sins—for which you were sorry. Being sorry for your sins certainly shows a measure of repentance. But when you have backslidden—especially if you have fallen in a way that brings Christ's name into disrepute— and you are earnestly wanting to be used again, I would have thought that a very deep repentance indeed is necessary.

This is why I would make the case that the repentance required of a returning backslider is deeper than what is required in saving faith.

This book, however, is not primarily designed to deal with the nature of conversion or saving faith but rather the restoration of one who has fallen but is a true Christian. The essential ingredient that promises restoration and future usefulness is a deep, heartfelt, genuine repentance. To put it another way, speaking personally, if I myself were a serious backslider and wanted assurance that I could be used of God to the maximum possibility, I would embrace the old Puritan definition of repentance. I would want to be sure that I have turned from every known sin. I would want this *not* for assurance of salvation, but to be as sure as possible that God would use me again.

But I would add this caution: beware of self-righteousness creeping in. When a person has fallen and comes back to the Lord, he or she sometimes develops a somewhat "holier-than-thou" attitude (if you can believe it). Yes, some people who have sinned greatly and get forgiveness for some reason seem to feel a need to compensate for the wasted time away from God. They sometimes become great "pointers of the finger"! It reminds me of a person I knew of who went on a diet and lost a lot of weight and then went around moralizing everybody he knew who was overweight! Don't let that happen to you. Unfeigned repentance combined with meekness and humility will put you in good stead to be used again.

The thesis of this book is this: God can use any fallen Christian, but on one condition—that he or she deeply repents. When there is a broken and contrite heart after a fall, there is hope.

True repentance is what builds a superstructure made of gold, silver, and precious stones. This, as I said in the previous chapter, is what David did after he submitted to Nathan's solemn word. He rebuilt a superstructure of gold, silver, and precious stones. The fall into sin—or the failure to walk in the light—is what builds a superstructure of wood, hay, and straw. It is only a matter of time until the superstructure will be shown for what it is. But when one sees the folly of building a superstructure that will not withstand the fire revealed at the judgment seat of Christ, there is something that can be done while there is time. That is to rebuild a superstructure, beginning with repenting truly and honestly. As long as there is life, there is hope. But as Thomas Fuller (1808–1876) put it, "You cannot repent too soon, because you do not know how soon it may be too late." Or as William Nevins said, "He that waits for repentance, waits for that which cannot be had as long as it is waited for. It is absurd for a man to wait for that which he himself has to do."

Three Greek Words for *Repentance*

There are basically three Greek words used in the Bible that may be translated "repentance." The first two are *metanoia* and *metamelomai.* The main one is *metanoia.* It means "change of mind," meaning the change of *nous*: "mind" or "understanding." The original Greek idea in *metanoia* was "later knowledge," "subsequent knowledge," often with the implication lest it be "too late." It is often said that we all have twenty-twenty hind-sight vision. To be granted repentance, a true change of mind is to have twenty-twenty vision *now* rather than later when it may be too late.

In other words, to repent means to see and do *now* what you will wish you had seen and done *later.* So if one is granted *metanoia* repentance, it is a marvelous mercy of a sovereign God.

It is being able to do what you will be glad you did, especially when you stand before God at the judgment seat of Christ.

Metanoia (the noun) is used twenty-four times in the New Testament. *Metanoeo* (the verb "repent") is used thirty-four times. It was central to the message of John the Baptist (Matt. 3:2, 8, 11), was used often by Jesus (Matt. 4:17; Luke 13:3, 5; 15:7, 10), and figured prominently in the preaching of the early church (Acts 2:38; 3:19; 17:30; 20:21; 26:20). It is said to be "granted" to the receivers, that is, *given*—not what you "work up" (Acts 5:31; 11:18; Rom. 2:4; 2 Tim. 2:25). In other words, it is either there or it isn't. It is precisely what some could not be granted "again," as in Hebrews 6:4–6, because they became stone deaf to hearing God's voice.

Therefore if one is given a true *change of mind* in time before it is too late, we have only to thank God and His undeserved mercy for this marvelous privilege. The worst scenario describes Esau, who could "bring about no change of mind, though he sought the blessing with tears" (Heb. 12:17). "He found no place of repentance" (KJV). This could refer to his being unable to change Isaac's mind, however, and may not necessarily refer to Esau's personal inability to repent.

What is absolutely certain, in any case, is knowing that God continues to give you and me true, honest, sincere, unfeigned, genuine, real repentance—a *change of mind* that comes before it is too late, vis-à-vis the scenario in Hebrews 6:4–6 when *metanoia* repentance does not come at all. Being changed from "glory to glory" (2 Cor. 3:18, KJV) is the same thing as being renewed unto *metanoia* repentance. We must prize this above all else in this world.

The second word, *metamelomai*, means "to experience remorse." Whereas *metanoia* implies that one has arrived at a different view of something, *metamelomai* indicates that one has a different feeling about it. This is the word used in 1 Samuel 15:35, that "the LORD was *grieved* that he had made Saul king over Israel." It is used in Psalm 110:4: "The LORD has sworn and will not change his mind" (cf. Heb. 7:21), that is, He will not regret His sworn oath. However, Paul uses both *metanoia* and *metamelomai* interchangeably in 2 Corinthians 7:7–10, which shows that one must not press the distinction of these meanings too far.

JUDAS ISCARIOT

Judas, one of the twelve disciples of Jesus, is in my view a type of the apostate, not a backslider. An *apostate* is one who at the end of the day turns against the Christian faith but was never truly converted in the first place. "They went out from us, but they did not really belong to us. For if they had belonged to us, they would have remained with us; but their going showed that none of them belonged to us" (1 John 2:19). I define a *backslider* as a true Christian—a person who has been truly converted but who falls—like King David. As C. H. Spurgeon would say, he falls not *off* the ship but *on* it. I would not say this of the apostate who never was on the ship in the first place.

One of the earliest threats to the Christian faith was Gnosticism (it comes from the Greek word *ginisko*, meaning "to know"). It was probably a pre-Christian philosophy that claimed a secret way of knowing but later imbibed part of the Christian faith. The Gnostics said, "We can make the Christian faith better with our own improvements." They had a defective teaching of the person of Christ (mainly denying His humanity) and were antinomian in both theology and conduct. *Antinomianism* (literally "against law") is a denial of any place of the Law in the

174

Christian life, often leading to lawlessness and immorality. Jude largely addressed the Gnostic threat and referred to those who were "blemishes at your love feasts, eating with you without the slightest qualm—shepherds who feed only themselves. They are clouds without rain, blown along by the wind; autumn trees, without fruit and uprooted—twice dead. . . . for whom blackest darkness has been reserved forever" (Jude 12–13). He had no doubt as to their final destiny. They were lost forever.

Peter also refers to them. He calls them false prophets, denying the sovereign Lord who bought them—"bringing swift destruction on themselves" (2 Pet. 2:1). Their punishment is certain. Moreover, "It would have been better for them not to have known the way of righteousness, than to have known it and then to turn their backs on the sacred command that was passed on to them" (2 Pet. 2:21). Jude says that they got into the church through the back door; they have "secretly slipped in among you" (Jude 4).

And yet Judas got in through the front door! Jesus actually chose him (Matt. 10:4). I don't know why, and I don't know anybody who does. It *may* be because Jesus wanted to set a pattern that shows not all who come into the church membership are truly born again. Judas was never born again. Jesus said early in His ministry, "Have I not chosen you, the Twelve? Yet one of you is a devil!" Then John added, that Jesus "meant Judas, the son of Simon Iscariot, who, though one of the Twelve, was later to betray him" (John 6:70–71). In other words, Jesus knew from the beginning who would betray Him. In His high priestly prayer, He said of the Twelve, "None has been lost excerpt the one doomed to destruction so that Scripture would be fulfilled" (John 17:12), referring to Judas. The King James Version calls him "son of perdition" (Greek *huios tes apoleias*). This indicates His final destiny, the same as we saw of the Gnostics above.

One further point: Judas "repented" that he betrayed Jesus. The Greek word here is from *metamelomai*, which the NIV translates "seized with remorse." This indicates that *metanoia* was not given to Judas. He was only sorry that he got caught or found out. Even if he did have a bit of a change of mind ("I have betrayed innocent blood"—Matt. 27:4), it came too late. Matthew does not dignify Judas's "repentance" with the word *metanoia*, the word generally reserved in the New Testament for true repentance. Matthew apparently wants to make the point that Judas was only sorry that things did not work out for him and the knowledge of his folly came too late. Remorse is often an essential ingredient in true repentance, but such a feeling can still be short of a true change of mind.

People will certainly have remorse in hell. But it will not be a repentance that is granted by the gracious Holy Spirit. Judas had remorse before he died and will have remorse forever in hell. One of the things that will make hell, hell is that people will have their memories in hell. The word came to the rich man who went to hell, "Son, *remember* that in your lifetime you received your good things, while Lazarus [who went to heaven] received bad things [on earth], but now he is comforted here and you are in agony" (Luke 16:25, emphasis added). Then the rich man requested that Lazarus be raised from the dead in order to warn his five brothers that hell really exists—and keep them from going there. The rich man assumed, "If someone from the dead goes to them, they will repent [Greek *metanoe-sousin*]" (v. 30). But the word came back—*no*. It is too late. The granting of *metanoia* will not come to those on *Earth* if they do not believe the Scriptures. God works through His Word to bestow repentance. So if people do not repent because they hear God's Word, neither will they be convinced even if one rose from the dead (Luke 16:27–31).

People will experience remorse as Judas did in hell.

In a word, Judas Iscariot was never converted in the first place.

A third Greek word used that is sometimes connected to repentance is *epistrophe*, which means "turning one's life around." This would mean turning from every known sin. Jesus said to Peter, "I have prayed for you, Simon, that your faith may not fail. And when you have turned back [Greek *epistrephas*], strengthen your brothers" (Luke 22:32). When Jesus said that Peter would need to be turned back or turned around, Peter couldn't believe what he was hearing and instantly replied, "Lord, I am ready to go with you to prison and to death" (Luke 22:33), whereupon Jesus predicted that Peter would deny Jesus three times. The point is, *epistrophe* is what characterized Peter's repentance after his fall. This word is not always used in connection with repentance, but the lesson from this is one the returning backslider needs to take on board. It would imply a much deeper and thorough repentance than the change of mind that might be assumed in *metanoia*. The returning backslider should therefore pray that he or she will be granted not only a change of mind but also a thorough turning around. A turning from every known sin is assumed in *epistrophe*. Any fallen person who wants restoration must return to the Lord in a depth of commitment and change of attitude and life that shows how strongly he or she feels.

INCESTUOUS SIN AT CORINTH

It must have grieved Paul deeply when he received word that one of his converts had indulged in a kind of immorality so horrible that it "does not occur even among pagans"

(1 Cor. 5:1)—namely, a man was sleeping with his stepmother. It is hard to say which probably upset Paul more—the incestuous sin or the cavalier attitude of his converts in Corinth. "And you are proud! Shouldn't you rather have been filled with grief and have put out of your fellowship the man who did this?" (1 Cor. 5:2).

At any rate, we have a scandalous fall of a believer in the church. This was a truly converted man, as we will see in more detail. Paul never questions whether the man who indulged in incestuous sin was saved; he questions the way it was handled, or, one should say, not dealt with at all by the church at Corinth. Therefore Paul rolled up his sleeves, stepped in, and exercised his apostolic authority and power:

> Even though I am not physically present, I am with you in spirit. And I have already passed judgment on the one who did this, just as if I were present. When you are assembled in the name of our Lord Jesus and I am with you in spirit, and the power of our Lord Jesus is present, hand this man over to Satan, so that the sinful nature may be destroyed and his spirit saved on the day of the Lord.
> —1 CORINTHIANS 5:3–5

This is very strong language. Paul said the same about Hymenaeus and Alexander (1 Tim. 1:20). When a professing Christian abuses the teaching of grace through faith, the world loves it. It dishonors the name of God, hurts the church's reputation, and discredits the gospel. Paul would prefer that people who do this not only be thrown out of the church but also released to the devil so that they will be destroyed and the damage done would be minimized.

Disciplining a church member is rare nowadays. I am not sure why. But when people who profess the name of Jesus lead

178

lives that openly dishonor His name, they should be confronted. Jesus put it like this, giving four steps (should all of these steps be needed):

1. Go to the "brother" (a saved person) who has sinned. "Show him his fault, just between the two of you. If he listens to you [by which Jesus means "if he repents"], you have won your brother over" (Matt. 18:15). That happy possibility would be the end of the story. No need to take it further or blab it to the world.

2. "If he will not listen [that is, if he does not repent], take one or two others along." The reason for this is to honor an ancient principle, that "every matter may be established by the testimony of two or three witnesses" (Matt. 18:16).

3. Take the matter to the church (Greek *ekklesia*— "the called out") if this sinning brother won't listen to a group of two or three. "Tell it to the church" (Matt. 18:17). This is open discipline and should embarrass the brother. But even then, said Jesus, this open rebuke may not work.

4. Excommunicate this person from the church. "If he refuses to listen even to the church, treat him as you would a pagan or a tax collector" (Matt. 18:17). That means he should not be treated as if he were in full harmony with the body of Christ. Let him go into the world and be utterly separated from the church.

Paul gave special advice to us when we see a fallen brother or sister. "If someone is caught in a sin, you who are spiritual should restore him gently. But watch yourself, or you also may be tempted" (Gal. 6:1). I love the way the King James Version puts it: "Restore such an one in the spirit of meekness." Having to confront a fallen brother or sister is an extremely delicate matter. It is like walking on the edge of a knife. The slightest wrong move could be disastrous. There is only one approach, says Paul. Approach such a person not with a harsh, judgmental finger-pointing, "how dare you do such a thing" attitude. You consider yourself—why? Because it could happen to you too! Remember the Golden Rule: "Do to others as you would have them do to you" (Luke 6:31).

Whenever it comes to you to approach a person who has fallen into sin, never forget that the same thing could happen to you. Even though you might not fall into the exact same sin as this man or woman has fallen into, you might fall into a rather different sin—but one that grieves the Holy Spirit just as much. Never forget that we all have feet of clay. There is not a single one of us who is exempt from sudden temptation. And Satan knows our weaknesses and knows how to arrange circumstances and events so that we will be most vulnerable. When you hear of *any* sin committed by another person, however disgusted you may feel at first, tell yourself, "There go I but by the grace of God." Because that is absolutely true.

When Paul ordered the Corinthians to deliver the man to Satan who committed incest, Paul may not have expected to see or hear of him again. As far as Paul was concerned, it was a *done deal*. It was over. But to quote Yogi Berra again, "It ain't over till it's over," and we have 2 Corinthians to thank for hearing the rest of the story. (We might wish there were a 2 Galatians in order to find out how things turned out in the Galatian church. But we will never know, as I said, until we get to heaven.)

Sometimes it is not merely an individual but a church that is required to repent. Jesus noted of the church at Ephesus that they had forsaken their first love. He then said to them, "Remember the height from which you have fallen! Repent and do the things you did at first. If you do not repent, I will come to you and remove your lampstand from its place" (Rev. 2:4–5). This church had fallen but not to the point of no return; they were given another opportunity to repent—as long as they could hear God speak! "He who has an ear, let him hear what the Spirit says to the churches" (Rev. 2:7). Thus the church at Ephesus had not reached a Hebrews 6:4–6 situation.

LESSONS FROM 2 CORINTHIANS

In 2 Corinthians we learn four things:

1. Paul's converts at Corinth obeyed his injunction.

He was relieved to hear that they did what he ordered them to do. "I wrote you out of great distress and anguish of heart and with many tears, not to grieve you but to let you know the depth of my love for you" (2 Cor. 2:4). Paul was thrilled to know that they did what he asked. He adds: "If anyone has caused grief, he has not so much grieved me as he has grieved all of you, to some extent—not to put it too severely" (v. 5). Paul added, "The reason I wrote you was to see if you would stand the test and be obedient in everything" (v. 9).

2. We learn that the punishment shook this man from the crown of his head to the soles of his feet—and he repented.

This was possibly unexpected but thrilling news. What must have turned this man around was to recognize it was a no-joke thing, that the apostle Paul categorically and unconditionally commanded that he be thrown out of the church and delivered to Satan—never to be seen again. It is the equivalent of Jesus's advice: "Treat him as you would a pagan" (Matt. 18:17). Had there been an attached condition, "But if you *do* repent later on, do come on back, and we will welcome you," I suspect the man would have weighed his options and not have been so shaken. It was the thought of *no hope* that got his attention. That was what stirred the people of Nineveh—Jonah gave them no hope whatsoever, only proclaiming that in forty days Nineveh would be destroyed (Jon. 3).

3. We learn thirdly that Paul said to take the man back into the church again.

"The punishment inflicted on him by the majority is sufficient for him. Now instead, you ought to forgive and comfort him, so that he will not be overwhelmed by excessive sorrow. I urge you, therefore, to reaffirm your love for him" (2 Cor. 2:6–8). This shows that this man *had* been granted a renewal of repentance and that he was not in a Hebrews 6:4–6 situation. It also suggests that the falling away in Hebrews 6 may not necessarily be a moral matter; the fundamental problem was that they could not hear God speak. And yet any number of sins—idolatry, immorality, grumbling, ignoring warnings from those over you, or any kind of disobedience—could lead to such stone deafness.

4. Finally, we learn the importance of total forgiveness.

"You ought to forgive and comfort him, so that he will not be overwhelmed by excessive sorrow" (2 Cor. 2:7). Then Paul adds, "I also forgive him" (v. 10). But now Paul adds an astonishing further reason for forgiving this man, however despicable his sin: "I have forgiven in the sight of Christ for your sake, in order that Satan might not outwit us. For we are not unaware of his schemes" (vv. 10–11). The Living Bible puts it like this: "A further reason for forgiveness is to keep from being outsmarted by Satan." This shows how crucial it is for us to forgive those who have repented. Not to do so gives Satan a certain authority he would not otherwise have. In other words, when I hold a grudge, point the finger, keep a record of wrongs, and refuse to let a person off the hook, it is on my part (even if unwitting) a beckoning for Satan to walk all over me. I do not want to do that.

We therefore have a mandate to forgive the returning backslider. This does not mean that he or she is necessarily given a platform. It is not essentially talking about being used again—at this point. But it *does* show how very important it is for you and me to hold out the olive branch to those who have fallen and have repented.

Our attitude to the returning backslider should be the same as the father of the prodigal son—and not like that of the older brother who resented the prodigal getting so much attention (Luke 15:25–30). I fear there are members of some churches who feel they have never done anything very wicked and who have so little graciousness toward a returning backslider. God hates this as much as He does the prodigal son's sin. As for the prodigal son, he was so fearful that he would never be allowed back into his father's good graces. One of the best definitions of repentance is put in the parable of the prodigal son to describe the prodigal's decision to turn from his old ways and ask for his father's mercy. What made him do it? Jesus said, "When he finally came to his senses ["came to himself," KJV]" (Luke 15:17). *That is repentance.*

As one of the church fathers, Ambrose (340–397) the Bishop of Milan, put it, "True repentance is to cease from sinning." The father's attitude when he saw his son coming home was the opposite of what the prodigal expected. Instead of running away from him, the father "ran to his son, threw his arms around him and kissed him" (Luke 15:20). The son said, "Father, I have sinned against heaven and against you. I am no longer worthy to be called your son" (v. 21). *That is repentance.* The father said to his servants, "Quick! Bring the best robe and put it on him. Put a ring on his finger and sandals on his feet. Bring the fattened calf and kill it. Let's have a feast and celebrate. For this son of mine was dead and is alive again; he was lost and is found" (vv. 22–24). The father's attitude should be the attitude of every one of us when we see the returning backslider.

I don't want to be unkind, but I cannot help but wonder if people who are biased against returning backsliders need to have repentance granted to them as much as the sinners they tend to judge. Immorality is sin; so too is self-righteousness.

If you feel that this chapter has been tailor-made for you, and if God grants you this level of deepest repentance, treat it as you would a vast fortune of gold, silver, and precious gems. For God granting true repentance means an invitation to rebuild a superstructure that will make all the discipline you have been through worth everything at the judgment seat of Christ.

"No," said Peter, "you shall never wash my feet." Jesus answered, "Unless I wash you, you have no part with me." "Then, Lord," Simon Peter replied, "not just my feet but my hands and my head as well!"

—John 13:8–9

Simon, Simon, Satan has asked to sift you as wheat. But I have prayed for you, Simon, that your faith may not fail. And when you have turned back, strengthen your brothers.

—Luke 22:31–32

I tell you the truth, before the rooster crows, you will disown me three times! Do not let your hearts be troubled. Trust in God; trust also in me.

—John 13:38–14:1

Peter was hurt because Jesus asked him the third time, "Do you love me?" He said, "Lord, you know all things; you know that I love you." Jesus said, "Feed my sheep."

—John 21:17

CHAPTER 10

SIMON PETER

T HIS FINAL CHAPTER IS DESIGNED TO DEMONSTRATE that a fallen person can be used again. I now write about my favorite disciple among the Twelve—the most famous and colorful. Simon Peter was a choleric, sanguine, take-charge type of person. He was devoted and unpredictable. "Wonderfully messed up," as Jeff Lucas put it. I am sure that under a lie detector, Peter honestly believed that he loved the Lord far more than *any* of the other Twelve did. When Peter was in the Spirit, he was in the Spirit indeed—truly brilliant, but when he was in the flesh, he was in the flesh indeed—not so brilliant! I suspect many Christians identify with Peter more than they do the other disciples, even if they are not born leaders.

Peter was the unofficial spokesman for the Twelve. "'Master, we've worked hard all night and haven't caught anything. But because you say so, I will let down the nets.' They caught such a large number of fish that their nets began to break.... When Simon Peter saw this, he fell at Jesus' knees and said, 'Go away from me, Lord; I am a sinful man!'" (Luke 5:5–6, 8). This shows the Holy Spirit at work, otherwise Peter would not have been conscious of his sinfulness. After that, Jesus issued the call: "From now on you will catch men" (Luke 5:10; Matt. 4:19). But it was Andrew who initially introduced his brother Simon to Jesus. "We have found the Messiah," Andrew told Peter, and brought him to Jesus, who looked at him and said, "'You are Simon son of John. You will be called Cephas' (which, when translated, is Peter)" (John 1:41–42). This was reaffirmed later after Peter confessed to Jesus—one of those times he was truly led of the Holy Spirit, "You are the Christ, the Son of the living God," and Jesus said, "You are Peter, and on this rock I will build my church, and the gates of Hades will not overcome it" (Matt. 16:16–18).

Jesus had His inner circle, comprised of three men who were let in on events that the others apparently knew nothing about—Peter, James, and John. On one of these occasions, Jesus took these three to a high mountain. Jesus was transfigured before them. His face shone like the sun, and His clothes became white. Moses and Elijah appeared on the scene, talking with Jesus. Peter said to Jesus, trying hard to impress Him, "Lord, it is good for us to be here. If you wish, I will put up three shelters—one for you, one for Moses and one for Elijah" (Matt. 17:4). This was not Peter's finest hour. Then a voice came from a bright cloud that enveloped them and said, "This is my Son, whom I love; with him I am well pleased. Listen to him!" (v. 5). They were terrified and fell face down to the ground. But when they were able to look up, they saw no one except Jesus—a loving rebuke from the Father that Jesus was greater than Moses or Elijah.

The same three men were allowed to witness Jesus raising a child from the dead (Mark 5:37–43). Peter, James, and John were also singled out to share in Jesus's dark hour in Gethsemane (Matt. 26:37).

All four of the Gospels tell of Jesus's prophecy that Peter would deny Him—and all four also describe the denial itself. But John's account adds a story not in the synoptic Gospels (Matthew, Mark, and Luke). It was during the occasion when

Jesus poured water into a basin and began to wash His disciples' feet, drying them with a towel He had wrapped around Himself.

Not one of the Twelve said a word against Jesus washing their feet, that is, until Jesus came to Simon Peter. Peter decided to exploit the moment to show he was different from the rest and that he loved the Lord more than these men did. So when Jesus came to Peter, in order to show that he was humbler and a cut above the others, Peter asked, "Lord, are you going to wash *my* feet?" (John 13:6, emphasis added). It was as though he were saying, "You don't really think I am going to let *You* wash my feet, do You?" But Jesus made it clear—yes, that is exactly what He intended to do. Jesus graciously replied to Peter, "You do not realize now what I am doing, but later you will understand" (v. 7).

At this stage, Peter was feeling really proud of himself. "'No,' said Peter, 'you shall never wash *my* feet'" (v. 8, emphasis added). He was sending a signal to all present—not only to Jesus but also the eleven, as if to say, "These men should be ashamed of themselves, Jesus, for letting You wash their feet; we should be washing *Your* feet." Peter was trying hard again to impress Jesus that he loved Jesus more than these men did; indeed, that he loved Jesus too much, respected Him too much, and valued His stature too highly to allow Jesus to lower Himself to wash their feet. How dare these men allow such a thing! "No, Lord, You will never wash *my* feet."

But Peter was soon put in his place. Jesus answered, "Unless I wash you, you have no part with me" (v. 8). Oh, dear!

Now Peter had to come up with a good one! He not only needed to save face for his pious protest but now outdo these less spiritual men in showing his superior love for Jesus. He thought he pulled it off: "Then, Lord...not just my feet but my hands and my head as well!" (v. 9).

I think this aspect of the life of Peter should send a signal to "pious" people who want the world to know how godly they are. Should this send a signal to you and me? Perhaps you don't need this, but I have to admit that I do. It is a timely reminder that I must not ever fall into the trap of overestimating how much I love the Lord.

It is like the Elijah complex. The ancient prophet sincerely thought he alone was left—that he was the only true prophet of God (1 Kings 18:22; 19:10). Elijah was wrong—very wrong. He completely forgot about Obadiah and the hundred prophets who had risked their lives in defiance of the wicked King Ahab (1 Kings 18:4). Not only that; in due course the Lord told Elijah that He had another seven thousand in Israel who had not bowed to Baal (1 Kings 19:18). Whenever we start feeling a little bit sorry for ourselves and imagine that we are so very important to God, He has a way of putting us in our place in order to keep us from taking ourselves too seriously.

So if you are among those who like to let people know how much you love God, then, more than ever, you should keep quiet about it. We should not even tell ourselves, much less others, how devoted to the Lord Jesus Christ we may think we are. This is why Paul said that he did not even judge himself (1 Cor. 4:3). Trying to assess how much we love God by how much we give, pray, or fast is the same thing as letting our left hand know what our right hand is doing. (See Matthew 6:1–18.)

Why? It is because a rebuke from God—one way or another— may be coming soon. And, God forbid, maybe even a grievous fall.

Jesus was getting ready to give Simon Peter the shock of his life. He was about to let Peter know what Peter would think unimaginable—that he would deny even knowing Jesus. But Jesus gently prepared him for this sobering forecast. It came immediately after a dispute arose among the Twelve as to which of them was considered to be greatest. Jesus stepped in and said, "The greatest among you should be like the youngest, and the one who rules like the one who serves" (Luke 22:26).

Peter had been right in the middle of this vehement discussion.

How do we know this? It is because Peter was immediately singled out. "Simon, Simon, Satan has asked to sift you as wheat" (Luke 22:31).

How did Jesus know that Satan had asked to sift Peter as wheat? Jesus had said, "The Son can do nothing by himself; he can do only what he sees his Father doing, because whatever the Father does the Son also does" (John 5:19). Jesus saw what was going on in the heavenlies, that Satan had to get permission from God before he could proceed to work through Peter. "Satan has asked..." He asked God the Father. You may recall that Job's trial was preceded by a conversation in heaven between Satan and God. Satan could do no more than God permitted (Job 1). So Jesus saw that Satan had his eye on Simon Peter. Nothing catches God by surprise. But it is interesting that all which followed—when Peter denied the Lord—was preceded by this eye-opening disclosure, namely, that Satan was behind the whole thing but within the permissive will of God.

You should know that if you are a chosen vessel, you are also a target of Satan. Jonathan Edwards said that when the church is revived, so is the devil. The closer you get to God, the more the devil will be aware of you.

Satan trembles when he sees the weakest saint upon his knees.

—WILLIAM COWPER (1731–1800)

My old friend Rolfe Barnard, now in heaven, used to preach a sermon called "The Man Who Was Known in Hell," basing it on the account of the seven sons of Sceva who were trying to cast out devils in the name of Jesus, saying, "In the name of Jesus, whom Paul preaches, I command you to come out" (Acts 19:13). They were actually trying to do something they were not at all qualified to do. And yet the evil spirit answered, "Jesus I know, and I know about Paul, but who are you?" (v. 15). Satan did not know these people!

The point that Rolfe Barnard wanted to make is summed up in his own words: "I want to be known in hell." That means that Rolfe would be a threat to the devil. I'm sorry, but so many Christians are no threat to the devil. Satan does not know about them!

Tell me, are you known in hell? Do you think that Satan is aware of you? Are you a threat to him?

Satan was aware of Peter. And when you have a calling and mission from God, Satan will want to interfere and abort that mission. Do you think that you could be a target of Satan?

Then Jesus added four things when He spoke to Peter in verse 32:

1. "I have prayed for you." There is nothing grander or more powerful than having the intercessory prayer of Jesus behind you. The moment Jesus said that, one could be assured of the ultimate outcome.

2. "That your faith may not fail." This was an implicit admission that Peter had faith. But faith can be

weak and not persevere. Peter had Jesus's prayer behind him, that his faith would persevere.

3. "When you have turned back," an implicit indication that Peter would have a fall but also that he would have a restoration. Jesus knew that His prayer would be answered, that Peter's failure would be temporary.

4. "Strengthen your brothers." This meant that Peter would resume the kind of leadership he was known to have among the other disciples, that he would be in a position to encourage them all.

Peter immediately replied, "Lord, I am ready to go with you to prison and to death" (Luke 22:33). Peter said that because he meant that. At Westminster Chapel we used to sing an English hymn: "O Jesus, I have promised to serve Thee to the end."[1] Peter promised this.

Then came the most stunning word Peter ever heard Jesus utter: "I tell you, Peter, before the rooster crows *today*, you will deny three times that you know me" (Luke 22:34, emphasis added). "Today." This seemed utterly preposterous. Peter insisted emphatically, "Even if I have to die with you, I will never disown you" (Mark 14:31). And all the other disciples said the same thing.

John's account is interesting. Keeping in mind that there were no chapters or verses in the original Greek, Jesus said to Peter, "I tell you the truth, before the rooster crows, you will disown me three times! Do not let your hearts be troubled. Trust in God; trust also in me" (John 13:38–14:1). The Greek is in the second person singular to Peter—"*you* will disown me three times," then he addresses all of them who had said they would not ever disown the Lord: "Let not your *hearts* be troubled." Jesus lovingly included the whole lot in His compassion.

In other words, He not only knew what Peter would do; He knew too that "all" the disciples would desert Him and flee (Matt. 26:56).

But the point is this. In the same breath that He told Peter that he would deny the Lord, He added, as it were, "Don't worry!" Amazing. "Do not let your hearts be troubled." It is as though Jesus said to them, "I know exactly what will happen, but it's *OK*—everything is under control."

God is never *really* disappointed. Displeased? Yes. Disappointed? No. It is because He knows the future as well as He knows the past. Moreover, He does not panic.

Imagine this! Jesus knows that Peter will fall but expresses His everlasting love the same moment! I call that *love*. When you know in advance that someone is going to let you down but love them just the same, it is a most remarkable matter.

But Jesus is that way with us. He knows if we are going to let Him down. But He loves us just the same.

The thing is, Peter didn't believe a word of it. And yet a few hours later—on the very same day—it all transpired. Jesus was betrayed by Judas, then arrested. He was taken to the high priest. A girl who was on duty asked Peter, "You are not one of his disciples, are you?" And would you believe it—Peter replied, "I am not" (John 18:17). It was cold. Peter was warming himself by the fire. He was asked for the second time, "You are not one of his disciples, are you?" The reply: "I am not." And then one of the high priest's servants challenged him, "Didn't I see you with him in the olive grove?" (John 18:26). According to Mark's account, it was at this stage Peter "began to call down curses on himself, and he swore to them, 'I don't know this man you're talking about'" (Mark 14:71). The rooster crowed. As the rooster crowed, the Lord turned and looked straight at Peter. Do not forget that Peter was looking at Jesus too. Their eyes met. Peter then remembered the word Jesus had spoken to him. "He broke down and wept" (Mark 14:72). "He went outside and wept bitterly" (Matt. 26:75; Luke 22:62).

I would have thought that the guilt Peter felt at that moment was incalculable. We can only imagine what depth of sorrow and shame he felt. But it was too late. All Peter could do now was lean on Jesus's unconditional love and trust those words Jesus spoke to be utterly and infallibly true.

But on Easter Sunday at the empty tomb, the angel instructed the women who came early in the day to anoint the body of Jesus: "Go, tell his disciples *and Peter*" that Jesus would see them in Galilee "just as he told you" (Mark 16:7, emphasis added). Peter was singled out in the initial message of Easter. It demonstrates the wonderful grace of God.

After Jesus was raised from the dead, ten of the disciples (Thomas was absent and Judas was out of the picture) were assembled in a room behind locked doors. They were afraid that the Jews might find them. You can be sure too that they, especially Peter, were ridden with guilt. Jesus unexpectedly came and stood among them. His words were: "Peace be with you!" The disciples were "overjoyed" when they saw the Lord (John 20:19–20). This joy came not only from the realization that He was raised from the dead but from having Him show up without moralizing them or making them feel the slightest bit ashamed. Instead of rebuking them and saying, "How could you have done this? After three years with you, you end up deserting Me! How could you?" There was not a hint of that. Their sin was pardoned so completely that it was as though they'd never sinned at all. Jesus's further words were, "Peace be with you! As the Father has sent me, I am sending you" (John 20:21).

The disciples were reinstated on the spot.

Later on, Jesus turned up at the shore of the Sea of Tiberias and prepared breakfast for the disciples. After they had finished eating, Jesus turned to Peter and asked, "Simon son of John, do you truly love me more than these?" (John 21:15). I interpret this to mean that it was Jesus's way of saying to Peter, who felt so embarrassed—unlike the rest, "Do you still think you love Me more than these do?" As we have seen, Peter always took for granted that he was the most devoted of the disciples. But this boast was taken away from him in one stroke.

As Peter disowned Jesus three times, Jesus asked Peter three times, "Do you love me?" Peter was hurt because Jesus asked him the third time, but he shouldn't have been. When we have failed our Lord, He has every right to test us.

The most incredible thing of all however is this: Peter has not only been forgiven and reinstated but chosen to preach the inaugural sermon of the church on the Day of Pentecost. One could presume that Peter would have been set aside to make room for a different disciple to preach—if only to discipline Peter further or question why Peter, who denied knowing Jesus only fifty days before, would be chosen so soon to be in such a ministry after his denial.

Simon Peter had already taken over as leader among the eleven during the waiting period in the Upper Room between Christ's ascension and Pentecost. Jesus had prayed that Peter would be able to strengthen his brothers. He was perhaps starting to do this. He stood up among the believers and took the view that somebody should replace Judas (Acts 1:15–26). Whether Peter was correct in his conclusion about Judas is debatable. But if you say, how dare Peter have such confidence and authority that he take the lead in this manner! The only answer is: he knew he was a forgiven man. Jesus totally set him free by the way Peter's denial had been foretold but also by the way Peter was given special attention by Jesus after His resurrection. So Peter was in no doubt.

Being without any doubt is what gave him such confidence on the Day of Pentecost. He even uses this word in his sermon: "Brothers, I can tell you *confidently* [Greek *parresias*— confidence, freedom, boldness]..." (Acts 2:29, emphasis added). This confidence, or boldness, is an essential part of the anointing, that phenomenon that an older generation used to call "unction" of the Spirit. Such power flows when you know, without any doubt, these things:

1. All your sins are totally forgiven.
2. What you are saying is absolutely, objectively true.
3. You have the undoubted approval of God.
4. You are the very instrument of the Holy Spirit, saying exactly what God wants said and nothing He doesn't want said.
5. The hearers are "cut to the heart" as they were on the Day of Pentecost (Acts 2:37).

But there is yet another reason that Peter was so effective on the Day of Pentecost. It is perhaps the main reason he had such power and acceptance with people. He did not have a trace of a judgmental or pompous attitude left in him. His self-righteous balloon had been punctured. He also knew that he was completely unworthy to be preaching that sermon. There was no pharisaical, arrogant, finger-pointing, condescending spirit in his personality or presentation; he was a transparent vehicle of the Holy Spirit. When one has grievously sinned but repented and been given infallible assurance of being totally forgiven, the result is, in a word, power.

I remember a particular Sunday morning in the pulpit at Westminster Chapel. I never felt so unworthy to preach in all my life. Louise and I had a big argument just before I had to leave for church. I slammed the door and pressed the button for the elevator. I was fuming. The next thing I know I am sitting on the large circular platform, bowing my head and looking spiritual. By then I had come to my senses. I thought, "Lord, there is no way I am going to be used today. I am unfit to be preaching." During the singing of the hymns I tried to get Louise's attention—to send a nonverbal signal, "I am sorry." But she did not make eye contact with me. There was no way I could send her a note—somebody might read it. I was simply shut up to the mercy of God. I never felt so much like a fraud. Never expecting for one moment to be blessed or helped in preaching, I just started quietly and slowly.

I couldn't believe what was happening. An extraordinary authority took over. I had liberty such as I had not known. The thoughts flowed. There was power there—but it wasn't me.

God was able to take over. He did. I was utterly out of the picture. I couldn't get over it. I went to the vestry and simply thanked the Lord with a profuseness and gratitude I had never felt. What is more, I thought of Peter when he preached at Pentecost. It came to me: "That's it. Peter was devoid of self-righteousness and filled with unworthiness, and that is why God used him, and why He used me today." Not that I was thankful for my abysmal attitude at home. Believe me, I apologized as soon as I got home (and was forgiven). But I was grateful for the lesson. I have tried ever since not to depend on my spiritual sense of preparation unless by that one means a feeling of absolute powerlessness and emptiness of oneself.

I am saying that Peter probably preached better than he would have had he not had the embarrassing fall at the very time the Lord was being handed over to the authorities. "All things work together for good to them that love God, to them who are the called according to his purpose" (Rom. 8:28, KJV). But one of the main principles of the truth of Romans 8:28 is this: the fact that something works together for good *doesn't mean it was right at the time the less-than-good thing happened.* God simply has a way of overruling by His grace and making things look good in the end. The good that results is the product of sheer grace, not that what we did was good or right.

Peter was a changed and new man. His fall did not keep God from using him.

LESSONS FROM PETER'S FALL AND RESTORATION

Things we must *not* conclude

We must be careful not to jump to conclusions regarding Peter's fall and restoration. One might read all I have said up to this juncture and come to a point of view we could not agree with at all. So let me mention five things you must not conclude about Peter's restoration:

1. Do not conclude that all who fall have a right to be used again.

Let no person say to God, "You used Peter after his fall; now You must use me!" We must not be so presumptuous. It is by the sheer grace of God that you have been forgiven and granted repentance. If you snap your finger and expect God to jump just because you believe you have fully repented, I would lovingly caution you that you seem to manifest a lack of humility and shame over what you have done.

The primary thing *all* of us are required to ask for when we pray is *mercy*. It is the way we were converted in the first place. "God, have mercy on me, a sinner" (Luke 18:13). Not only that; none of us ever outgrow the need for mercy. It is what each of us must first obtain when we pray, no matter what our condition. "Let us then approach the throne of grace with confidence, so that we may receive *mercy* and find grace to help us in our time of need" (Heb. 4:16, emphasis added). When you ask for mercy, you have no bargaining power; you have nothing you can give to God in exchange. God can give or withhold mercy and be absolutely just either way. God said to Moses, "I will have mercy on whom I will have mercy" (Exod. 33:19).

When we realize we have no claim or right to be used of God at all—much less used *again* after a fall, our first step should be asking for His mercy.

On the other hand, when you consider that God used Peter again—and the awfulness of what he did—this should encourage anybody who has fallen! Scandalous behavior doesn't get much worse than this—outrightly cursing and denying that he even *knew* the Lord Jesus. Imagine that. Some sins are worse than others, and Peter's sin—short of blaspheming the Holy Spirit (denying that Jesus is God in the flesh)—is as bad as it gets. And yet God forgave him, restored him, and used him wonderfully. But Peter knew better than anybody that he had no right to have a second chance. Neither does any of us.

All we can do is ask for *mercy*.

**2. Do not assume that those who will be used again only
need to wait fifty days after their failure.**

It would be foolish for anybody to think like this. The
shortness of time between Peter's failure and his remarkable
preaching on the Day of Pentecost has been used by some as
a reason they "don't need to wait two years" or whatever the
length of time may be. First, it is hard to believe that a person
is sincere in his or her repentance who would expect to be used
so soon—especially when they *demand* to be used! I'm not sure
that Peter even expected to be used again. He had surely elimi-
nated himself from usefulness. But God overruled.

I must repeat, when we have failed the Lord Jesus Christ by
bad behavior, we have in that moment forfeited any "right"—
if we ever really had one—to be used by Him after that. It is
therefore ludicrous—silly—to use the fifty-day time period as a
pattern for how long a person should wait before being brought
back into ministry.

There is no definite time scale we can count on. Each situation
should be dealt with and considered on a case-by-case basis.

**3. It is a mistake to think that those who fall should not
have to worry about further disciplining.**

It could be argued by some that Peter did not undergo any
discipline at all for his denial of Christ. There was no judicial
court, panel, or committee that passed judgment on Peter. And
when Jesus appeared to him after the Resurrection, there was no
hint that Peter ought to be disciplined before he was launched
into ministry.

I answer: ecclesiastical structures had not been set up. Peter's
failure came before there was any time or need for church
government as such. It is dishonoring to God to bypass the

godly opinions of those whose responsibility it is to look after the church and the honor of God's name.

4. It is foolish to think that those who fall will not have to face the consequences of their sin.

First of all, Peter faced the consequence of what he did the moment he heard the rooster crow and saw the look of the Lord straight at him. He sobbed his heart out. He would have given a thousand worlds not to have done what he did. He would have to live with that forever. And yet his denial of Jesus did not result in the horrendous kind of hurt and sorrow that comes to a spouse, family, church, and community as a result of, say, sexual sin.

The fact that God forgives our sin implies no hint that we do not have to live with the consequences of our sin. God forgave David. But not only did the child die who had been born to Bathsheba, but the pain and sorrow in David's heart and life, not to mention the fallout in David's family, continued on and on for years. We all have to live with the consequences of what we have said and done even though our sins have been washed away by the blood of Jesus Christ.

5. Do not think that those who fall and are restored will also be exalted overnight.

It is true that Peter was restored and catapulted to a high profile within a very few days. He became the most talked about figure in Jerusalem for a good while. But this is owing to the circumstances of the day that are not likely to be repeated. Yes, God can do anything. But there are some things He will not do during your lifetime or mine: He will not make two and two equal five or make a rock so big He cannot lift it. We all have to live within the perimeters of the culture and society into which we have been born and whom we must reach.

Things we may safely conclude:

1. All who fall can be forgiven.

Never forget that good old promise, "If we confess our sins, he is faithful and just and will forgive us our sins and purify us from all unrighteousness" (1 John 1:9). It cannot be stressed enough that *all* manner of sin and blasphemy (except the blasphemy of the Holy Spirit) is pardonable.

Peter's being forgiven is encouragement to us all. Take the matter of witnessing to the lost. Have you ever failed to witness to a lost person because you feared what the reaction of that person or other people might be? This *could* be the very equivalent of Peter's sin. God will forgive you for this. Not only that; He forgives the worst possible sins—all those that come under the scrutiny of the Ten Commandments. Sins against the Ten Commandments and Jesus's interpretation of them in the Sermon on the Mount are *all* forgivable.

Never forget: Jesus will not break the bruised reed (Matt. 12:20). I am sure that Jesus felt just as keenly and deeply for Peter as Peter felt for himself when the crowing of the rooster was heard. I would not press this too far, but perhaps it hurt Jesus more than it hurt Peter just to have to watch Peter weep as he did.

2. We are all loved with an everlasting love.

What was true of ancient Israel is true of every born-again child of God: "I have loved you with an everlasting love" (Jer. 31:3). Jesus never stopped loving Peter in all he did. There was nothing Peter could have done to make Jesus love him more and nothing he could have done to make Jesus love him less. We are loved with an everlasting, perfect, and unconditional love.

3. God is still married to the backslider.

When God rebuked Israel for their waywardness and backsliding, He still said, "I am your husband" (Jer. 3:14). That has not changed. We are the bride of Christ. God hates divorce (Mal. 2:16) and practices what He preaches! Since we are the bride of Christ, God is determined to present us faultless in the end (Eph. 5:27; Jude 24). In the meantime, He rebukes and chastens us (Rev. 3:19).

If God is the husband, He is the head—and provider. He will look after us in every detail.

4. God can use anybody.

I say this fully aware that God can overrule every principle I am outlining in this very chapter. I have given my cautions. But God is not bound by anything I say in this book, no matter how much I want to be (and hope I am) led by Scripture.

Church history is riddled with exceptional cases and unusual people—who seem to break all the rules. I myself resisted being ordained for a good while because my hero Charles Haddon Spurgeon was never ordained. He said: "Their empty hands on my empty head will not add to my empty ministry." But one day I had a stark revelation—I'm not Spurgeon! So I submitted to ordination.

If there is any message I would be pleased to convey—and be remembered for most of all—it is this: God can use anybody. If He could use Peter, Moses, Jonah, David, Judah, or Gideon, He can use me. And believe me, dear reader, if God can use me, He can use anybody.

5. All who anticipate being used again must repent as sorrowfully as Peter did.

Peter did not weep bitterly because he knew cameras were focused on him or because he thought this scene would be written up and remembered forever. His sense of shame was private, personal, and knew no bounds. What he felt in those moments—and for days (and, for all I know, for the rest of his life)—could have never been adequately described.

If you have fallen and expect to be in ministry again, there must be a combination of *metanoia* (change of mind), *metamelomai* (remorse), and *epistrophre* (turning around). It must also be an irrevocable, a no-turning-back state of the mind, heart, and will.

Whoever you are, if God has granted you repentance, I can promise this: God isn't finished with you yet. He would not have *granted* you repentance had He not envisioned a future for you. I don't know all that this means for every reader, but, after all, God is no respecter of persons, and He loves you as much as He loved Simon Peter.

Final Thoughts on Peter

Peter wasn't perfect after his restoration. Acts 10 reveals that he had deep theological and cultural biases that had to be cleansed and dealt with. Until he saw God deal sovereignly with Cornelius, he thought Jews were a cut above everybody and that a Gentile had to become a Jew before one could be truly converted (vv. 34–35, 47). Almost certainly, you and I have a lot of theological baggage left that needs to be cleansed and dealt with too—I guarantee it. I pray to discover my own as soon as possible. But I will need a final discovery and thorough working over of all I have believed and preached that was not totally sound—in heaven. I just hope I don't have to wait that long!

Paul let us in on a rather unpleasant aspect of Peter—once. Paul had to chide Peter for abruptly excusing himself from Gentiles when he saw certain Jews coming along. This is terrible! He didn't want fellow Jews to see him being friendly to Gentiles! "I opposed him to his face," said Paul, "because he was clearly in the wrong." Peter had apparently been intimidated by Judaizers (Gal. 2:11–12)—Jews who professed faith in Jesus but who may not have even been converted. So Peter was far from perfect, even after he had been greatly used of God.

When Saul of Tarsus became the apostle Paul, this news was not always warmly welcomed by some Hebrew Christians. I look forward to watching a video replay of so many things when we get to heaven! But "all's well that ends well." Peter granted in the end that Paul's writings, though "hard to understand," were to be recognized as Scripture (2 Pet. 3:16). Peter accepted Paul—but only just!

Finally, God did a wonderfully gracious thing to Peter. God gave him a second chance to show he was unashamed of Jesus. It came when Peter and John were summoned before the Sanhedrin. They were flogged and then ordered not to speak in the name of Jesus (Acts 5:40). I can imagine how some in the Sanhedrin must have been thinking: "We showed them; this will teach them a lesson; they have been punished and humiliated. We won't have to be bothered with them again. They are now sorry for what they have done." Or words like these.

The truth is, Peter and John were so excited and thrilled they had to pinch themselves that they could be so blessed. Whereas most people I know dread any kind of shame or humiliation—for any reason—all I know is that Peter and John left the Sanhedrin "rejoicing because they had been counted worthy of suffering disgrace for the Name" (Acts 5:41). Peter let God down the first time, but not this time; moreover, it took place before powerful Jews, not merely a servant girl.

Think about that phrase: "counted worthy." Who counted them "worthy"? God did. What a privilege it was to be "counted worthy" to suffer shame for Jesus! That is exactly the way they felt. It was Peter's second chance. He was so grateful that he had a second chance to stand up for the name—and not blow it this time. God is so gracious.

If God can use Peter with all his weaknesses and biases, He can use you and me.

And we know that all things work together for good to them that love God, to them who are the called according to his purpose.

—Romans 8:28, KJV

CONCLUSION

I SUPPOSE EVERY AUTHOR LIKES TO THINK THAT HIS OR her latest book is their "best yet." I also suspect, if they are Christian writers, they like to think every word they wrote was inspired. One of my publishers told me of one of their authors who refused to let an editor tamper with his material because "God wrote it."

I can assure you, God did not write this book! *I did.* I do not hold God responsible for the material in this book! I can only say with certainty that I *asked* God for His help. I wrote it from my heart and experience—which goes back over fifty years. My first pastorate began in March 1955 at the Church of the Nazarene in Palmer, Tennessee.

As I close, I want to make five final suggestions:

1. Let God decide whether you will be used again.

We can come up with our formulas and recipes for restoration, but at the end of the day, it is up to God whom He restores, reinstates, and gives a second chance to engage in ministry. I think that He decides on a case-by-case basis, so be willing to wait at the end of the line. Wait until your name is called. Also ask yourself: would I want restoration equally as much if there were no financial blessing attached?

Wait, then, until you are asked to return. When you first entered the ministry, did you not at first receive an invitation? When God comes to a person a second time, He who *recommences* a good work will complete it (cf. Phil. 1:6). Wait for the invitation, however long it takes. If it never comes, can you leave things in God's hands? My loving counsel: don't rush things; don't manipulate. Don't promote yourself. "No one from the east or the west or from the desert can exalt a man. But it is God who judges: he brings one down, he exalts another" (Ps. 75:6–7).

2. Value your own personal relationship with God above a public ministry.

At the judgment seat of Christ, about which this book has had a lot to say, it will be your personal relationship with God that will matter most. Esteem intimacy with your heavenly Father above anything else. If getting into the ministry means more to you than becoming more like Jesus and knowing Him, I would have to say to you in all candor: you should not be in ministry. At least, not yet.

3. If someone comes to you, taking a hard line that God will not use you again, you have a right to ask by what authority do they make such a pronouncement.

I hope I am not being ungracious, but such a position smacks of a pharisaical interpretation of Scripture—not one that mirrors a God of tenderness toward bruised reeds. I also cannot help but ask how might their position change if *they* or someone they *love* should, in the future, fall into the very trap they have condemned.

It would seem that God is more gracious than some.

What I know is this: God has chosen to fill up the Bible with all kinds of shady, broken, failed people who exemplify His amazing willingness to receive them back when, like the prodigal son, they "come to themselves."

4. Whether God offers to restore and reinstate you or not, begin now to devote the rest of your life to rebuilding a superstructure of gold, silver, and precious stones.

This means a life of sexual purity, transparent integrity, genuine meekness, a heart devoid of bitterness, and a will not bent on vindication.

5. If by the grace of God you are restored, avoid a self-righteous spirit.

Never judge those who led to your exposure. Be sympathetic with Christians who are slow to accept you.

> *May the blessing of the triune God—Father, Son, and Holy Spirit—be upon you for the rest of your life. Amen.*

Notes

What Others Are Saying...
1. Johann Heinz, *Justification and Merit* (Berrien Springs, MI: Andrews University Press, 1984), 217–218.

Introduction
1. R. T. Kendall, *The Judgment Seat of Christ* (Scotland: Christian Focus Publications, 2004).

Chapter 2
Ending Well
1. R. T. Kendall, *The Sensitivity of the Spirit* (Lake Mary, FL: Charisma House, 2002).
2. R. T. Kendall, *How to Forgive Ourselves—Totally* (Lake Mary, FL: Charisma House, 2007).
3. "Love Divine, All Loves Excelling" by Charles Wesley. Public domain.

Chapter 3
God's Blueprint
1. "My Hope Is Built" by Edward Mote. Public domain.
2. Ibid.

Chapter 4
The Quality of the Superstructure
1. "Like a River Glorious" by Frances Ridley Havergal. Public domain.
2. R. T. Kendall, *Controlling the Tongue* (Lake Mary, FL: Charisma House, 2007).

CHAPTER 5
MONEY AND SEX

1. Peter Baker and John F. Harris, "Clinton Admits to Lewinsky Relationship, Challenges Starr to End Personal 'Prying,'" *Washington Post*, Tuesday, August 18, 1998, Page A01. http://www.washingtonpost.com/wp-srv/politics/special/clinton/stories/clinton081898.htm (accessed June 20, 2007).

2. R. T. Kendall, *Is God for the Homosexual?* (Basingstoke, UK: Marshal Pickering, 1988).

CHAPTER 6
POWER

1. William Shakespeare. *Measure for Measure*, 2.2, http://www.shakespeare-literature.com/Measure_for_Measure/6.html (accessed July 3, 2007).

2. R. T. Kendall, *God Meant It for Good* (Waynesboro, GA: Authentic, 2007).

3. R. T. Kendall, *Total Forgiveness* (Lake Mary, FL: Charisma House, 2002); *How to Forgive Ourselves—Totally* (Lake Mary, FL: Charisma House, 2007).

CHAPTER 7
THE MIGHTY FALLEN

1. R. T. Kendall, *The Anointing: Yesterday, Today, Tomorrow* (Lake Mary, FL: Charisma House, 2003).

2. M. A. Eaton, *Preaching Through the Bible: Genesis 12–23* (Kent, England: Sovereign World, 1999), 77.

CHAPTER 8
THE RETURNING BACKSLIDER

1. "Lord, I'm Coming Home" by William J. Kirkpatrick. Public domain.

2. R. T. Kendall, *A Man After God's Own Heart* (Scotland, UK: Christian Focus, 2001).

CHAPTER 10
SIMON PETER

1. "O Jesus, I Have Promised" by John E. Bode. Public domain.

If you have been encouraged and challenged by R.T. Kendall in *God Gives Second Chances,* here is another book we think you will like.

Are your words getting you into trouble?
It doesn't have to be that way!

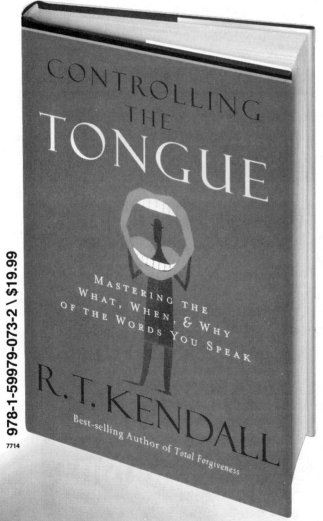

In his engaging teaching style, Dr. R.T. Kendall demonstrates how to take control over what you say. Learn how to master that unruly tongue and reap eternal reward.

978-1-59979-073-2 \ $19.99

7714

Visit your local bookstore today!

FOL
AUG 3 1 2023